DATE DUE

EDUCATION WITHOUT COMPROMISE

William D. Schaefer

EDUCATION WITHOUT COMPROMISE

From Chaos to Coherence

in Higher Education

Jossey-Bass Publishers

San Francisco • Oxford • 1990

EDUCATION WITHOUT COMPROMISE
From Chaos to Coherence in Higher Education
  by William D. Schaefer

Copyright © 1990 by: Jossey-Bass Inc., Publishers
                       350 Sansome Street
                       San Francisco, California 94104

&

                       Jossey-Bass Limited
                       Headington Hill Hall
                       Oxford OX3 0BW

Library of Congress Cataloging-in-Publication Data

Schaefer, William D.
    Education without compromise: from chaos to coherence in higher
education / William D. Schaefer.
        p. cm. — (Jossey-Bass higher education series)
    Includes bibliographical references (p.).
    ISBN 1-55542-197-0
        1. Education, Higher—United States—Aims and objectives.
    2. Education, Higher—United States—Curricula.   I. Title.
    II. Series.
    LA227.3.S32   1990
    378'.01'0973—dc20   89-43459
                                                                     CIP

Manufactured in the United States of America

The paper in this book meets the guidelines for
permanence and durability of the Committee on
Production Guidelines for Book Longevity of the
Council on Library Resources.

Credits are on page 155.

JACKET DESIGN BY WILLI BAUM

FIRST EDITION

Code 9008

The
Jossey-Bass
Higher Education
Series

Consulting Editor
Teaching and Learning

Kenneth E. Eble
University of Utah

Contents

Preface

Although in recent years a goodly number of books have been written on education—a few of them, astonishingly, best sellers—I feel that even the best have skirted, or have failed to recognize, some of the most important issues. No one would deny that there are problems in our educational institutions, nor, in light of recent publicity, need one be "in education" to list many of them. All of us—parents, teachers, school administrators, public officials—have expressed concern over the low scores on standardized verbal and math tests, the high number of high school dropouts, the low level of funding for elementary and secondary schools, the increasingly high cost of higher education, and the low (and ever-lowering) quality of teachers and teacher training—to mention just a few of the more highly publicized issues. And we have surely been right in so doing.

Still, I believe that such concerns, legitimate as they undoubtedly are, have tended to obscure some even more important issues. Were these the only problems—and had we world enough and time (and money)—education in America today could presumably be "fixed." But I would argue that we are ignoring some very basic problems different in both kind and degree of importance, and that the situation is even more serious than the public has been led to believe.

I would argue, for instance, that we face a far more serious problem in that many of our four-year colleges and most of our universities—as well as virtually all of our secondary schools—have mindlessly mixed vocational and academic courses without continuity or coherence or anything approaching a consensus as to what really should constitute an education. This is, to me, a *basic* issue—one that goes to the heart of the matter and that can be addressed only through deliberation and determination, not dollars. I believe that we should be, but are not, deeply concerned about this confusion of purpose—a confusion that has led colleges and universities to make fraudulent claims about their goals and missions as they package a hodgepodge of unrelated courses and incoherent requirements into a so-called liberal arts degree. And there are other issues of similar importance. I believe, for instance, that it is essential at all levels of education to cease playing games with the teaching of communication skills, especially in institutions of higher education, where instruction in reading and writing is more often than not disdained or demoted to the status of "remedial." I fear that in our definition of academic disciplines, in the academic organization of our colleges and universities, and consequently in our academic programs, we have failed to come to terms with a knowledge explosion that is promising to change the substance of education. And I think that we could go a long way toward restoring integrity to the college classroom were the humanistic and some of the social science disciplines to reconsider the extraordinary emphasis they currently place on publication of scholarly drivel—an obsession that has diminished the classroom experience and has cheated generations of unsuspecting students. It is to issues such as these that this book is addressed, in asking that we rethink the college curriculum and restore meaning to the liberal arts degree—indeed, reconsider the very substance of higher education—and in so doing begin to offer our students what I am calling an "education without compromise."

Although I harbor the hope that professional educators and academic administrators will read my book—a few, perhaps, with more than passing interest—my remarks are not directed exclusively or even primarily to an academic audience. Believing that we in academia too often speak only to ourselves—failing to recognize or perhaps unwilling to admit that changes in education seldom occur without public understanding of the need for change—I have written primarily for that somewhat enigmatic and oft-maligned creature, the educated layperson, and for students and teachers of any age who are in the process of becoming one. While I have occasionally referred to monographs, reports, and newspaper articles that over the years have crossed my desk, my book is not a scholarly treatise with its authority predicated on reference to other authorities or to the classic texts on educational theory. It is largely based on my experience working in and around institutions of higher education over the past forty years—as a student at seven colleges and universities, a teacher at four universities, the author of several scholarly books and (as we say in the profession) numerous articles and reviews, the editor of a prestigious scholarly journal, and an academic administrator who has served as executive director of the largest professional association in the humanities and as academic vice-chancellor of a prominent research university.

Consequently, my book is part history and part auto-biography, and as such I necessarily draw most heavily on the field (literary studies) and the institutions (UCLA, Wisconsin, NYU, Columbia, Chicago) with which I am most familiar. It is a subjective, impressionistic, anecdotal compilation of personal reflections—in essence, a collection of informal essays. But while as essays each chapter can more or less stand alone, the book has a logical progression: it moves from broad to more narrow concerns, from a consideration of an issue that involves all levels of education to some specific problems in higher education and finally to several issues primarily concerning the humanistic disciplines. Although these issues are in many ways related, *Education Without Compromise* has no overriding theme or message beyond that suggested by its title, nor does it attempt to provide solutions to all of the issues it raises. I will have achieved my purpose if my reflections merely help to focus attention on the problems I have chosen to address and thereby lead to further discussion.

Overview of the Contents

In my first chapter ("Education Today"), I begin by taking a broad view of the educational process and suggest that we have gone astray in attempting to merge—without definition, sequence, structure, or coherence—very different kinds of educational objectives. I see this as being true not only in our elementary and secondary schools but also in our undergraduate programs, in which, or so I argue, academic "education" and not vocational instruction or training should be the goal. In the second chapter ("Liberal Education"), I elaborate on this idea by explaining what I believe we mean, or at any rate should mean, by a liberal education, and I discuss what we can and cannot expect students to gain from experiencing it. I try to explain the reasons for our failure, especially in large public universities, to provide a meaningful "general education" for undergraduates, and I conclude with a description of what I believe might be done to make our efforts more successful. In my third chapter ("The Knowledge Explosion"), I build on these ideas by suggesting that as we struggle to redefine the canon, revise the curriculum, and rethink what we mean by a liberal education, we are ignoring monumental changes that have occurred during the past fifty or so years and that have led to a proliferation of new—and a blurring of old—academic disciplines. I attempt to show how these new disciplines and a growing array of "interdisciplines," instead of revitalizing education, as they well might, have at present merely complicated and confused scholarship and teaching. I further suggest that the organization of academic units in most colleges and universities currently fails to accommodate changing times and has become, or is rapidly becoming, a deterrent to a liberal education.

Following on an idea developed in my first chapter—
the idea that education of whatever kind or quality must
begin with the acquisition of communication skills—in my
fourth chapter ("Reading and Writing"), I discuss the teaching of composition at the postsecondary level. I examine what
has happened to college writing programs over the past few
decades and suggest that we will continue to have a literacy
crisis in our colleges and universities, as well as among college graduates, until we recognize college writing courses as
an important and a legitimate, not a remedial, part of the
curriculum. This discussion leads to the next chapter ("Other
Languages"), in which I deplore the fact that most college
students, including those with advanced degrees, are unable
to communicate in languages other than English. I expand
on my belief that even limited skills in a second language,
if studied with the goal of attaining proficiency rather than
merely meeting a course requirement, can immensely enrich
the educational experience. I also suggest that the major reason language instruction in colleges and universities has been
less successful than it might be is that it is usually taught in
language departments in which, ironically, the teaching of
the language is not the primary concern.

In my sixth chapter ("Teaching and Learning"), I
reflect on changes that have and have not occurred with students and teachers in the past half-century and develop my
idea that students today lack intellectual curiosity primarily
because they have not been taught how to be taught and
because, for the most part, they do not understand what a
liberal education really means. In my seventh chapter ("Publishing, Perishing"), I examine the inane stress currently
placed on scholarly publication in the humanistic and some
of the social science disciplines—a preoccupation that has
led to a reward system focused on dissemination of ideas in
print rather than on exchange of ideas in the classroom. And
in Chapter Eight ("Humanities Today"), I consider how over
the past twenty years humanities departments, in becoming
"professionalized," have isolated themselves and their subjects
from the public, while at the same time public perceptions of

the humanistic disciplines have been perverted through the efforts of the National Endowment for the Humanities (NEH) to "promote" and "sell" the humanities. Indeed, as defined and publicized by NEH, *humanities* is a word that has become so generalized (and pompous) as to demean the importance and distort the reality of the humanistic disciplines.

In my final chapter ("Summing Up"), I examine some of the good and some of the bad things that have of late occurred in the humanistic disciplines and in higher education, and I try to explain why I believe that the humanities must hold a central position in what throughout the book I describe—in opposition to training—as "education."

Acknowledgments

During the seventies and eighties, I spoke hundreds of times in cities at home and abroad on a range of subjects having to do with higher education and the humanities. Many of these papers have been published and occasionally republished, although usually in such obscure journals that only a handful of academics, mainly those teaching in the humanistic disciplines, have been exposed to them. In writing this book, I have drawn on portions of these papers, including a few of those in print, without acknowledgment.

I must also note that while many of my examples are drawn from my experience in the English department at UCLA, I will be sadly misconstrued if my comments are interpreted as an attack upon my colleagues or my university. UCLA is today one of the truly distinguished research universities in this country, and its department of English is, I believe, second to none in both its graduate programs and its undergraduate teaching. The problems I discuss are national in scope, involving virtually all colleges and universities. That they exist in the best of institutions makes them even more frightening.

I owe an immense debt of gratitude to many wonderful people with whom it has been my privilege to work these past forty or so years. Because some of the most wonderful would be distressed at a number of things I have to say in this book and might wrongly be accused of guilt through association, they shall be nameless. I do, however, want to acknowledge the invaluable assistance of Gale Erlandson, higher education editor with Jossey-Bass, and the advice of Professor Kenneth Eble, whose comments on earlier versions of this book influenced my thinking and whose untimely death prevented me from adequately thanking him for his help.

Los Angeles William D. Schaefer
December 1989

The Author

William D. Schaefer is professor of English at the University of California, Los Angeles (UCLA). He attended the University of Missouri (1945–47), Los Angeles City College (1948–49), Yale University (1949–50), the University of Chicago (1950–51), and New York University (1956–57), from which he received his B.A. (1957) degree in English. His master's (1958) and Ph.D. (1962) degrees, both in English, were earned at the University of Wisconsin, where as a teaching assistant he was given an award for distinguished teaching. In 1961–62 he received a Fulbright grant to London, where he spent the year completing his dissertation.

In 1962 Schaefer joined the faculty of the department of English at UCLA and from 1969 to 1971 served as chairman of his department. In 1971 he was granted an extended leave of absence to serve as executive director of the Modern Language Association (MLA) in New York, an office he held until 1978. At that time he returned to UCLA and for the next nine years was the executive vice-chancellor, the chief academic officer of the university. In 1988 he rejoined his department where, after a seventeen-year hiatus, he has resumed his teaching career.

xix

From 1968 to 1975 Schaefer was associate editor of *Nineteenth-Century Fiction* and, during his years with the Modern Language Association, was editor of *PMLA* and general editor of MLA publications. He has held visiting professorships at New York University and Columbia University and has served on a number of national boards.

Schaefer has written numerous articles on higher education and the humanities, and, prior to his years in administration, published scholarly articles and reviews in *Victorian Studies, Victorian Poetry, Nineteenth-Century Fiction,* and *PMLA.* A specialist in Victorian literature, he is also the author of two books: *James Thomson (B. V.): Beyond "The City"* (1965) and *The Speedy Extinction of Evil and Misery: Selected Prose of James Thomson (B. V.)* (1967).

EDUCATION
WITHOUT
COMPROMISE

❦ 1 ❧

EDUCATION TODAY

Our Chaotic Curriculum

Somethin' tells me
It's all happening at the zoo.
I do believe it,
I do believe it's true.

The monkeys stand for honesty,
Giraffes are insincere,
And the elephants are kindly but
They're dumb.
Orangutans are skeptical
Of changes in their cages,
And the zookeeper is very fond of rum.

Zebras are reactionaries,
Antelopes are missionaries,
Pigeons plot in secrecy,
And hamsters turn on frequently.
What a gas! You gotta come and see
At the zoo.

—Paul Simon

One of the most basic problems in education today stems from a lack of agreement, a clear consensus, as to what it means or could mean for someone to be "educated." On some of our larger school and college campuses, where the side-shows dominate the activities in the main ring, it seems that what we have resembles a circus. But when I view education nationally and at all grade levels, seeking but not finding a

1

philosophical rationale or logical coherence part to part and
parts to whole, I conclude that education in America today is
very like a zoo.

That faculty are skeptical of changes in their cages,
administrators plot in secrecy, and some students "turn on"
frequently is no doubt true, but that is not what I have in
mind with my analogy to a zoo. Nor is it that we find in our
schools and colleges reactionaries and missionaries, the honest and the insincere, or even an occasional zookeeper who
is excessively fond of rum. My point is that we have placed
within the educational zoo virtually every conceivable subject
on earth—all of God's creatures—with the implication that
education can mean just about anything we want it to mean.
Tigers and trigonometry, monkeys and mechanics, llamas
and languages, flamingos and finger painting, elephants and
electives. And electives. And more electives. You gotta come
and see.

I begin at the beginning by suggesting that there are
three, and only three, basic ingredients in the educational
process—the teacher, the student, and the subject. The process
can therefore be reduced to a simple X-Y-Z formula. A teacher
(X) knows something or knows how to do something (Y) that
someone else, a student (Z), would like to know or know
how to do, or needs to know or know how to do for his
or her comfort or survival. Thus X teaches Y to Z. And
although the elaborate substructures and superstructures we
have through time created around our formal educational
institutions sometimes overwhelm this simple X-Y-Z process,
the fact remains that other parts of the educational zoo—
departments of education, governing boards, school princi-
pals and college presidents, professional associations and
accrediting agencies, textbook publishers and testing services,
admissions officers and student counselors, alumni organizations and football teams—are peripheral and exist, at least in
theory, only to facilitate the occurrence of that singular act
whereby X teaches Y to Z.

Because the act is a natural one, engaged in, albeit with
varying degrees of complexity, throughout the animal king-

dom—informally in the crib or nest, in a more structured
way at work or play, formally in what we call formal education—we "in education" can take consolation in the realiza-
tion that nothing we do will prevent it from occurring, be it
under the bamboo tree or in the halls of Harvard. And one
can at least hope, even under present conditions, that there
will be instances where the educational process as an organized activity actually succeeds—instances where informed,
well-prepared teachers present a coherent program of instruction to a group of dedicated students who fully understand
what they are studying and why. Such instances are, unfortunately, isolated and increasingly rare. Par for today's course
is a so-called educational institution in which we find many
teachers who are less than competent, students neither committed to nor prepared for receiving instruction, and a con-
glomeration of unrelated courses dedicated to the proposition
that one's reach should never exceed one's grasp. And how
else could it be without a consensus, a plan, an agreement
as to what we are trying to do, and why? The elephants are
kindly, but they're dumb.

The more I have pondered this problem, this confusion
of purpose and goals, the more I have come to believe that
in large part it results from a failure to distinguish among
different categories of teaching, of which I fancy I have identified three that are fundamental and into which all kinds of
teaching can be grouped.

My first category has to do with communication, an
educational goal in and by itself but, at the same time, a
prerequisite to the educational process: whatever the goal, it
is necessary for teachers and students to establish a means
through which information can be conveyed. There are, as
always, exceptions. One can, for instance, be self-taught by
observing the actions of others without any direct or indirect
communication between teacher and teachee, and there is
apparently something similar to the learning process that
occurs through genetic transfer ("fish gotta swim; birds gotta
fly"). But the educational process I am discussing requires
that teacher and student develop a means for communication,

share a "language," and this is true whether the teacher be a person or a machine, whether the student be human or canine, whether the vehicle for communication involve sight, sound, touch, or any of the senses. Communication skills are truly the basis of education, and the degree of complexity, subtlety, or sophistication involved in the means of communication largely determines the potential for success in teaching the subject at hand.

My dog, Androcles, and I can, for example, communicate at a basic level through the makeshift language I have taught him (and he me) by drawing on a number of the senses. With this language we can satisfy certain of our desires—mainly visceral on his part, largely egocentric on mine—and can communicate to the point where I am able to teach him to do a variety of things—catch a ball, shut the door, fetch the newspaper, sit.

The educational process breaks down, however, because of the limitations in our method of communication. It is a classic case of the sensitive, caring teacher (me) and the dedicated, motivated student (Androcles) lacking an adequate means for sophisticated communication. Consequently, not only am I unable to teach my dog to do things more constructive than catching, shutting, fetching, and sitting, but we have no way to discuss the things I have been able to teach him, no way to relate them to each other, to seek out their deeper meaning, to *think* about these things. Androcles, for instance, "knows" death. In his Rhodesian Ridgeback heart he somehow understands the thing that is and then is not, but we have no language through which we can analyze that most intriguing phenomenon. The basic communication skills are inadequate, and thus we are condemned to a rather crude, if wonderful, relationship that mainly involves pointing and petting, wagging and woofing.

Canine concerns aside, and turning to our two-footed friends in the elementary schools, I trust we would all agree that to function effectively in a modern society one must acquire certain elementary skills. It is useful, for instance, to be able to read and write or at least to speak a language—

preferably, in this country at this time, the English language. And surely all of us involved in education are aware that our mission includes teaching basic skills, however defined, recognizing that with the three R's, regular brushing habits, and a little bit of luck one can indeed prosper in this society. But—and here I think we begin to get into trouble—those "basics" that we are eternally obsessed with getting back to are also a prerequisite for advanced studies. The problem is that, lacking an idea of the totality, innocent of the student's ultimate goal, we have failed to develop a coherent sequence of instruction to ensure that a student will build on the basic foundation, will eventually master the advanced skills that are essential for higher, much less highest, education.

In 1983 the College Board published a pamphlet with the promising title *Academic Preparation for College: What Students Need to Know and Be Able to Do.* But while this pamphlet lists the obvious subjects and for each attempts to describe what it persists in calling the "outcomes" of a secondary school education, it fails to define with any degree of precision the quality of those "outcomes," the level of sophistication students must attain in each area if their college education is to be meaningful. What we have are thousands, tens of thousands, of kindly teachers trying to do good deeds, trying to improve the skills of a group of young people they have inherited from other kindly teachers who have been trying to do the same thing. And there are of course examinations and grades and diplomas, but in reality it is all quite arbitrary. Thus we find, for example, that at the University of California nearly half of the entering freshmen—students who are among the upper eighth of the state's high school graduates—are unable to read or write at a level that would enable them to deal with complex ideas; that more than a third are unprepared to take the freshman-level mathematics course essential for their advanced studies in the sciences; that only a small fraction have been taught how to see rather than just look at a painting, how to hear rather than merely listen to the sounds of music. That standards at the University of California may be somewhat higher than at other state-supported

institutions is irrelevant. I am talking about the basic foundations, the fundamental skills, the tools of education without
which students have limited opportunities for a satisfying
life, much less a realistic hope of ascending any educational
ladder, a fact that today is less than obvious because, as I have
been arguing, most of our educational ladders have not been
placed in the upright position.

In any event, having established an effective means of
communication at an appropriate level of complexity, the
educational process can continue and, in its initial form, will
inevitably involve "training." This is a word that, for lack
of any better, I assign to my second category, teaching to *do*
something. Those cavepersons who through sign and sound
created a language that could be understood by younger cavepersons undoubtedly taught the first courses in how to do
something, teaching a particular skill necessary to accomplish a specific task. Thus in the beginning we had "Fire
Building 1A," "Slaying the Saber-Toothed Tiger 1B," seminars (with field trips) in "Managing the Mammoths." Because
such training was useful, enabling the survival of the species
while immensely improving the standard of living, it caught
on. As it was in the beginning, so is it now, so will it be
forevermore. The student does not know how to do something. The teacher does. The teacher teaches.

In this kind of education, teaching is designed to result
in an action. The act may be as simple as tying one's shoes,
as complicated as performing open-heart surgery. Sometimes
the thing one desires to learn to do is frivolous, such as hang-
gliding or performing card tricks. More often it is related to
one's livelihood: hunting or fishing in a less complicated
world, computer programming or genetic engineering in our
present civilization. As such, we call it "vocational" or "professional" education. From birth through Berkeley we engage
in this kind of instructional process, limited in our aspirations only by talent, intelligence, and the degree of sophistication we have attained in those basic communication skills
essential for mastering whatever the task at hand. All well
and good, but by no means all.

For returning to our hairy ancestors in the caves, it seems that once upon a time some kindly caveperson was inspired to revise the curriculum by adding a course in "Cave Painting." What was it, that strange, new, unproductive, possibly subversive activity? It did not, I think, have anything to do with interior design, much less a desire to create a thing of beauty that would be a joy forever. It was, I believe, the expression of a desire to understand the meaning of all the things that cavepersons did or had done in the past, and of all the things that had been done to them by powers not themselves. It was a desire to connect—man with mammoth, feast with famine, past with present, life with death—and thereby to attempt to comprehend the universe. It was "education" in its quintessential form, "knowing" as opposed to "doing," "knowing" not because one necessarily can or need do anything with the knowledge but because it is important in and by itself, because knowledge is better than ignorance, light is better than darkness.

And this desire leads to my third category of teaching: that through which the heroic odes, the transcendent myths, the classical traditions, the knowledge of the ages, no less, have been learned and taught, and learned and taught again, from generation to generation through pictures, song, story-telling, books, and, more recently, film. This is the stuff of "education" as opposed to vocational training—history and anthropology, psychology and biology, all the "ologies" involved in the sciences and social sciences, and, to be sure, the study of art, music, theater, dance, literature, religion, philosophy. These are the subjects that comprise a liberal education, that inform a civilized society, that lead to understanding and, one might hope, eventually to wisdom. For many if not all of us who teach in schools and colleges, this is what it is all about; this is what we signed on for as keepers of the flame.

Learning to know. Learning to do. Learning to communicate in order to know or to do. Three different categories of teaching, three different kinds of learning experience. Trying to make it real, but failing to do so because we have taken these very different kinds of educational objectives and have tossed them all together in our educational zoo, allowing the students to wander pretty much where they will. It is education without definition, without sequence, structure, or coherence. And it is not, of course, of recent origin. My own public school education in the thirties and forties was, and I fear still is, typical.

The standard form used for reporting a student's progress in the eleven elementary schools in my hometown had three main headings—mental growth, social growth, and physical growth. Physical growth was taken literally, each report card faithfully recording my height and weight as I advanced in stature if not necessarily wisdom. Social growth was measured through a bizarre combination of geography, history, civics, promptness, courtesy, and self-control. And a student's mental growth was evaluated within three categories, with applied arts (music, drawing, manual, and household) given equal status with language arts and with mathematics and science. As a result, while I have only vague memories of studying mathematics and science or language arts, of acquiring the skills and knowledge essential for moving from elementary to secondary instruction, I can vividly recall setting type by hand in a printing class, carving bars of Ivory soap into what for me always came out looking like frogs, and, in a woodworking class, making a pump lamp, the pump handle pulling the chain that sometimes (not often) lit the lamp. This curious mixture of the sacred and profane continued through high school, where in my freshman year my studies in English, Latin, and algebra were mingled with industrial arts, chorus, and physical education, and in my senior year history, economics, and trigonometry with typing, creative writing, and the ubiquitous physical education. That was and, although the names may have changed, basically still is public school education—a jumble of unrelated, undifferentiated courses that leave the students confused, if not curious, as to what it was all about. Paul Simon's "Kodachrome" puts it this way:

> When I think back
> On all that crap I learned in high school,
> It's a wonder
> I can think at all.

But while this situation exists today from the most elementary of elementary schools right on through our high schools and junior colleges, to grasp fully the enormity of the situation one must turn to a four-year college or university catalog, any catalog. Take mine, for example, at the University of California, Los Angeles, where to earn a baccalaureate degree the undergraduate student selects 45 out of several thousand courses, some 250 of which will satisfy the "general education" requirement that is intended to ensure "breadth." UCLA is, of course, a major research university, and thus you will find no courses in cosmetology, no "Wordprocessing for Nonmajors." But we do have "Metamorphic Petrology" along with "The Evolution and Dynamics of the Nursing Profession." We have "Combinatorial Algorithms" along with "Fundamentals of Exposition," "Biomechanics of Musculoskeletal Injury" and "Group Dynamics in Sport," "Intermediate English as a Second Language" and "Advanced Sanskrit," "The Design of Specific Polymeric Systems" and "Chinese Brush Painting," "The Crisis of Consciousness in Modern Literature" and "The Taxonomy and Ecology of Ornamental Plants." The undergraduate curriculum itself is a zoo. Bits and pieces, fragments shored against our ruin, kindly, but oh so dumb.

I exaggerate, of course, exaggeration being a kind of poetic license for one who fancies that, like Tiresias, he has seen it all already. One who is subject at times to despair, suspecting not infrequently that education, like youth, is wasted on the young. But one who is deeply concerned that we have compromised education by continuing to send generations of young people through this zoo until their time stops and we hand them a diploma, waving fond farewells while we know full well that the majority of those kids are

semiliterate, largely unskilled, ignorant of even the existence
of entire disciplines, and thoroughly confused as to why they
came in the first place.

Some years ago a Sunday issue of the *New York Times*
included a sixteen-page advertising supplement titled *Why
Go to College?* (Alexander, 1980). Published by the Professional Staff Congress, the union representing the instructional staff of the City University of New York (CUNY),
the report began by explaining that by going to college
"You'll Be Prepared for a Career." The next section was titled
"You'll Have a Better Chance of Getting a Job," and, as one
was informed on the following page, "You'll Have a Better
Chance of Getting a Good Job." The next section listed in
some detail "Where Jobs Will (and Won't) Be in the 80's,"
and the following section, with an appropriate graph and
table, documented the idea that "You'll Have a Better Chance
of Earning More." Only at the conclusion of the report,
almost as an afterthought, was space devoted to the idea that
"You'll Be Better Prepared for a Fulfilling Life": college, at
least at CUNY, promised to provide—not necessarily an education—but better health, richer leisure, self-confidence, the
ability to cope, and family success (college-educated people,
one was astonished to learn, experience a higher degree of
marital happiness than others).

This ad is a classic, my favorite example of the confusion we have created in the minds of students and parents as
to what a college education is all about. The claims are of
course fraudulent, an outrageous instance of the selling of a
college education based on nonsense. In a society where in
measuring success the high school diploma has been replaced
by the baccalaureate degree, one obviously has less opportunity to obtain an attractive entry-level job without a degree,
however meaningless the college experience. That is a given.
But that in a four-year undergraduate degree program most
colleges effectively train a student for a career any more than
they provide a student with a broad-based liberal education
is simply not true. In attempting to accomplish both they in
fact succeed in neither.

I should perhaps make it clear that I have nothing against jobs. They are good and good for you. But if the reason for pursuing postsecondary education is to get a job, then, depending on one's aspirations, one should either go to a vocational school, of which there are many (including the armed forces), or earn a baccalaureate degree and then enroll in a graduate program at a university. For in their graduate programs universities are primarily—in most cases, exclusively—involved in job training, providing a no-nonsense vocational education for those who aspire to be doctors, lawyers, chiefs; or architects, engineers, dentists; or physicists, chemists, biologists; or even university professors. From Oxbridge onward, vocational education is, and always has been, what a graduate degree is all about.

For graduate students, the educational process is, in fact, pure "training," in that it is designed to help students acquire the skills and knowledge necessary to gain employment in whatever field they have chosen to pursue. And this is true whether the job they seek will involve practical application of the skills and knowledge attained (that is, "doing" something outside academia as a "trained" professional) or whether it will be a job involving basic research, within or outside of academia. If one's field is research in the sciences or health sciences, positions are of course available in commerce and industry; but more often than not, and especially if the field is in the humanistic disciplines, the student will seek employment in a college or university. Consequently, perhaps the most specialized job training that goes on in a university is that which a graduate student undertakes in one of the humanistic disciplines, given that the educational experience (ignoring the realities of the marketplace) is directed toward only one kind of job opportunity, teaching—a subject on which I will have more to say in a later chapter.

For the faculty who teach in those large public and private institutions that award the highest professional as well as academic degrees, the distinction between "education" and "training," between theory and practice, is not merely one of confusion but at times one of conflict, with internecine

warfare easily breaking out over allocation of funds, assignment of faculty positions, and decisions in personnel cases.
Sociologists who work in social welfare programs are sometimes viewed by the "real" sociologists as rank amateurs,
psychologists in schools of education are often accused of
doing "bad science" by those who hold positions in psychology departments, and English professors frequently disdain
work done on the major dramatists by those who teach in
theater departments. Perhaps the most extreme example of
this conflict between theory and practice, between "education" and "training," occurs in the fine arts. Art historians
seldom have nice things to say to or about the practicing
artists on their campus, and studio artists tend to think of art
historians as meddlers who would have no idea what to do
with a canvas and paint brush. Historical musicologists frequently view with contempt those who work in the performance areas, and those musicians who perform and teach
performance have little patience with the historians.

Moreover, even within a school whose primary mission
is to produce professionals, there are programs leading to
both "practical" degrees (the M.B.A. in the business school,
the J.D. in law school, the M.D. in medical school) and the
"academic" degrees of master of arts, master of science, or
even doctor of philosophy. In the medical school clinicians
mingle with colleagues who have no clinical interests and are
engaged in basic research; in business schools accountants
and theoretical economists are found on the same faculty;
and in schools devoted to public health one finds both epide-
miologists, who frequently do research much like that undertaken by basic scientists in a biology department or a medical
school, and health administrators, whose concerns are closer
to those of certain faculty in schools of business management
or schools of education. The research university is therefore a
curious hybrid on which extraordinary demands are placed
to accommodate activities ranging from the most theoretical
to the most practical.

Were graduate programs and those who teach graduate
courses unrelated to undergraduate programs and undergrad-

uate students, this conflict would not be especially harmful—
would not, in fact, be unlike the competition (for the most
part healthy competition) that occurs among the various constituencies in any business organization. That is not, however,
the case in most universities, where the graduate faculty not
only teach undergraduates but, consciously or unconsciously,
tend to shape the undergraduate curriculum in light of their
graduate teaching and their professional or research interests.
Even while championing the importance of scholarship in
graduate education, Jaroslav Pelikan, former dean of the graduate school at Yale University, has had to admit that when
the graduate school's definition of scholarship "makes its
presence felt within the work of the college teacher, it can
fundamentally distort the commitment of the undergraduate
curriculum to the aims of general education" (1983, p. 12).

Thus for undergraduates who genuinely desire to pursue a liberal education—and happily there still are such
students—conflict and confusion in the graduate programs
exacerbate their problems as undergraduates, not only as
regards the curriculum but because in many instances those
broad-based introductory courses in cave painting are reluc-
tantly taught by faculty whose real lives are concerned with
finding a better way to manage the mammoths. It is not so
much that we are what we teach but that we tend to teach, or
teach around, what we do, which is why when undergraduate
students, after complaining that they never get to take courses
taught by the "name" professors, frequently wonder what all
the fuss was about when they do. Obviously research and
teaching are not always or necessarily incompatible, nor are
professional and academic interests. One could name a number of Nobel laureates as well as practicing professionals who
are also superb in a freshman or sophomore introductory
course. Unfortunately, these are exceptions.

The combination of vocational and academic education
in graduate schools is, in any case, inevitable, as it obviously
is in public elementary and secondary schools. Given the ideal
of a free and mandatory public school education for America's
large and diverse population, to track children into purely

vocational or purely academic programs based on early testing would be unacceptable. I accept that. But what I am arguing in this chapter and throughout this book is that an undergraduate college education need not and should not reflect this confusion of purpose and goals, that undergraduates in a four-year college or university should receive an academic education, not vocational instruction. Yet unless and until the confusion between these two kinds of educational experience is understood by all concerned parties and academic education is recognized as the exclusive province of an undergraduate program, students and their parents will continue to believe that the underlying purpose of a college degree is primarily if not solely to enable one "to get a better job."

As David Riesman (1981) has reminded us, at some point in the past two decades higher education has shifted from a period of near-total faculty hegemony to an age of student consumerism, where what is taught, and even how it is taught, is increasingly dictated by student expectations. Acknowledging those expectations, institutions of higher education have themselves increasingly encouraged—and with the extraordinary growth of the two-year colleges have virtually assured—a particular kind of student expectation: one that is essentially pragmatic. Little wonder, then, that between 1969 and 1984 the percentage of undergraduates who believe that "training and skills for an occupation" are the most essential outcomes from a college education increased from 59 percent to 73 percent, or that when 1,000 college-bound seniors were recently asked about their reasons for wanting to attend college, 90 percent replied, "To have a more satisfying career," an opinion echoed by 88 percent of their parents (Boyer, 1987, pp. 11-12, 67).

What I believe is missing is a clarification of the process itself, so that students and their parents will understand what are fundamentally very different kinds of educational experience and will know precisely what kind is being offered where, when, and why. When I say that as a nation we lack a clear consensus as to the meaning of education, that we in effect lack an *idea* of education, what I am really saying is that we have too many ideas, all of which we attempt to pursue simultaneously, frequently in the same institution, without differentiation or clarification. High school students may be immature and insecure, but they are not, by and large, unconcerned when it comes to their future. They do have aspirations, even if, as is so often the case, those aspirations are sadly limited by a limited awareness of the choices. If we were to clarify those choices, if we were to define more clearly the nature of the institutions—vocational school, proprietary school, junior college, four-year liberal arts college, university—to which they think they aspire and then tailor their high school programs to prepare them for the kind of educational experience they choose to pursue, we would by no means have fixed American education, but I believe we would have imposed some sense of sequence and some degree of coherence to it.

Change begins with awareness, and, as regards the possibility of focusing undergraduate education on "education," there is some cause for hope: for I sense that there is today a greater degree of restlessness, a more profound dissatisfaction with education, than at any time in the past half-century. The orangutans are, to be sure, still skeptical of changes in their cages, but I like to think that throughout the educational kingdom there is a dawning awareness that there is something fundamentally wrong with our system. One encouraging symptom of this is the renewed and highly publicized interest in strengthening the liberal arts curriculum in colleges, with the implication that students might be better off were they to receive on-the-job training in their chosen profession after graduation. And there is, in fact, some indication that businesses are looking increasingly to liberal arts graduates rather than to those with professional majors. This encouraging development is discussed thoroughly in a 1986 study titled *Educating Managers: Executive Effectiveness Through Liberal Learning*, a book that "urges a central role for liberal learning in the development of current and future managers as a matter of simple good sense and enlightened self-interest on the part of businesses and those who lead them" (Johnston and Associates, p. *xiii*).

I recently heard the vice-president of a large corporation admit that he prefers to hire, not accounting majors or M.B.A.'s, but B.A.'s with a degree in English. "You can teach a group of Cub Scouts to do portfolio analyses," he claimed, no doubt correctly, but what he wanted was people "who can read and speak in the language we're dealing with." Indeed, a recent survey of some 3,000 business leaders revealed that in the hiring of new employees, reading ability, reasoning skills, and personal enthusiasm rank far more importantly than technical training (Boyer, 1987, p. 105). And while many students fear that a liberal arts major, especially in a humanistic discipline such as history or philosophy, may be less attractive to corporate recruiters than, say, a major in engineering, a survey of recent graduates at the University of Illinois reveals that this is not the case at all. While, not surprisingly, at the time of graduation 83 percent of the engineers were employed, compared to only 38 percent of the liberal arts majors, after nine months the percentages were nearly identical—98 percent for the engineers and 94 percent for those with liberal arts degrees. Moreover, five years after receiving their bachelor's degrees, 87 percent of those who had majored in the liberal arts were satisfied with their careers and 85 percent claimed that, if given the choice, they would again major in the liberal arts (Boyer, 1987, pp. 269-270).

Some years ago I clipped, and have since cherished, an editorial from the *Wall Street Journal* written by a senior vice-president of the American Can Company, who put it this way: "For its executives of the future, business will want to select from a cadre that is diverse and versatile. It will want MBAs and engineers and communicators, sociologists and historians and even a philosopher or two. It will need dreamers and realists and pragmatists, drivers and moralists. It will want candidates with imagination and organization, confidence and humility. Above all, business needs people who are smart, who know how to use their brains and how to work well with others" (Alexander, 1981, p. 16). That, I would argue, is a call for a liberal education, not vocational training.

My plea for coherence and continuity, for a clarification of purpose and goals in education, is hardly new. In claiming that as we allow our undergraduates to select mindlessly from thousands of largely unrelated courses we lack an *idea* of education, I am reminded of a series of lectures written some 135 years ago by John Henry Newman and published under the title *The Idea of a University*. Newman—in another time, another place—also pleaded for a "liberal," as opposed to what he called a "servile," education and succinctly described the kind of program we were even then beginning to package and have now perfected, turning our students into

> earnest but ill-used persons, who are forced to load their minds with a score of subjects against an examination, who have too much on their hands to indulge themselves in thinking or investigation, who devour premiss and conclusion together with indiscriminate greediness, who hold whole sciences on faith and commit demonstrations to memory, and who too often, as might be expected, when the period of education is passed, throw up all they have learned in disgust, having gained nothing really by their anxious labors except perhaps the habit of application. . . . [They] leave their place of education simply dissipated and relaxed by the multiplicity of subjects, which they have never really mastered, and so shallow as not even to know their shallowness. How much better is it, I say, for the active and thoughtful intellect, where such is to be found, to eschew the College and the University altogether, than to submit to drudgery so ignoble, a mockery so contumelious! [Newman, (1852) 1960, pp. 112–113].

I could not have said it better myself.

❧ 2 ❧

LIBERAL EDUCATION

The Great Pretender
in Today's
Colleges and Universities

Only connect! That was the whole of her sermon.
Only connect the prose and the passion, and both will
be exalted.

—E. M. Forster

Our concern with the quality of undergraduate education is
hardly new. It is, in fact, as old as undergraduate education.
In the past ten years, however, a number of reports and studies highly critical of American colleges and universities have
renewed and heightened interest in the topic. Indeed, since
1977, when the Carnegie Foundation for the Advancement
of Teaching pronounced that general education in American
postsecondary institutions was a "disaster area," criticism of
the baccalaureate degree has become a national pastime. We
have been told that the curriculum is a junkyard littered with
the reforms of five decades, that colleges offer a smorgasbord
of courses from which students pick and choose their way to
graduation, that the standards for a baccalaureate degree have
come to vary so greatly that no one can say what the degree is
supposed to represent, that we have reached the point where
we are more confident about the length of a college education
than its content and purpose, and that the chaotic state of
the baccalaureate curriculum may be the most urgent and

18

troubling problem of higher education in the final years of the twentieth century. (See Boyer, 1987, p. 83; Boyer and Hechinger, 1981, p. 6; Bennett, 1984, p. 19; Association of American Colleges, 1985, p. 2; and many others.)

To earn a baccalaureate degree in an American college or university (as opposed to many foreign institutions [Clark, 1985]) a student accumulates a specified number of credits by satisfactorily completing a certain number of courses. Approximately one-third of these courses are taken within a field of specialization (the major), one-third may be electives (sometimes involving a minor), and the remaining one-third, usually selected from a long list of courses in the sciences, social sciences, arts, and humanities, are required to ensure that the student, in theory, receives a "general education." Although the recent publications on undergraduate education cover a good deal of territory, most of the criticism has been directed to this third component—to general education, which, according to the 1987 study by the Carnegie Foundation for the Advancement of Teaching, is today "the neglected stepchild of the undergraduate experience" (Boyer, 1987, p. 83). Yet it is, I believe, this part of an undergraduate education that consumers (students, parents, taxpayers) mainly have in mind when they want to know what a baccalaureate degree means. They want to know what knowledge and skills students will have acquired after four years at a particular college or university that will have made them educated in ways different from (and implicitly better than) those who attended a different institution, pursued a vocational education, or did not go to college at all.

What most of the recent studies are calling for, then, however they might differ in detail or emphasis, is the establishment (or reestablishment, revision, redefinition, reconsideration, reorganization) of the general education part of undergraduate degree programs. That some 95 percent of all colleges and universities already require completion of a core of general education courses (Boyer, 1987, p. 87) suggests that the problem is not a failure to provide such an education but that what is currently being offered is outdated, inadequate, ineffective, inconsistent, or incoherent. One can choose one's own adjectives. Any and all will probably apply to most such programs as they exist today.

Although we have recently been told by Allan Bloom (1987) that colleges and universities are guilty of closing the American mind, impoverishing the soul, and failing democracy, to describe the present situation as a disaster is perhaps a bit excessive. Nevertheless, in pondering this issue I am reminded of Auden's description of the fall of Icarus as depicted in Brueghel's painting, where the boy, having flown too close to the sun, his wax wings melted, is shown falling into the sea. The plowman on shore tends to his plowing and the ship—a merchant ship, I fancy—sails on. Auden described it this way:

> How everything turns away
> Quite leisurely from the disaster; the plowman may
> Have heard the splash, the forsaken cry,
> But for him it was not an important failure; the sun shone
> As it had to on the white legs disappearing into the green
> Water; and the expensive delicate ship that must have seen
> Something amazing, a boy falling out of the sky,
> Had somewhere to get to and sailed calmly on.

Because general education is usually the foundation for what schools call a liberal education, the terms are frequently used interchangeably. It is not uncommon, however, to find some kind of a general education requirement even in an institution that offers primarily vocational training, and thus I differentiate between the two terms by considering "liberal education"—which in my first chapter I have simply called "education"—to describe the totality of an undergraduate program. Such an education differs from vocational training in that it has no object beyond itself. It is its own justification, its own reason for being. It involves curiosity, the desire to acquire knowledge simply for the sake of knowledge. It involves, however we choose to define them, the "Great

Books." It is what Matthew Arnold called Hellenism as opposed to Hebraism, "knowing" instead of "doing." It means learning the best known and thought in this world so as to establish a climate for new and fresh ideas. It fulfills what Arnold liked to call the "need in us for Greek," the ability to see life steadily and to see it whole. It is "pure" education, without compromise.

There are, however, limitations in a liberal education—limitations that, if unrecognized, frequently lead to false expectations and unrealistic assumptions, among them the belief that those who acquire such an education will not only be wiser but in some indefinable way will be better than those who do not. Great books, with or without capital letters, can indeed provide a kind of packaged experience, a heightened experience that in a variety of subtle and not-so-subtle ways has the potential for enriching our lives. A liberal education does not, however, guarantee goodness. There is no reason to believe that the well-read individual, even the college English professor, aspires to sainthood. There is, I would say, a fifty-fifty chance that the person who has read with care all of Wordsworth's poetry will be somewhat more likely than others to be kind to our friends in the woods, but I would not push it much farther than that. Some of my best friends in the humanistic groves of academe do not wear halos.

Moreover, in spite of Shelley's claim that poets are the unacknowledged legislators of the world, experience suggests that Auden comes closer to the truth when he asserts that poetry—and the study of poetry, and literature, and history, and philosophy, and all of the "ologies"—makes nothing happen. I refer to Auden's splendid elegy to William Butler Yeats, where, addressing Yeats, Auden says,

> You were silly like us: your gift survived it all:
> The parish of rich women, physical decay,
> Yourself; mad Ireland hurt you into poetry.
> Now Ireland has her madness and her weather still,
> For poetry makes nothing happen.

Auden goes on, however, to imply something else in this poem: the idea that while poetry (and, I would add, all of the above) may appear to make nothing happen, it continues to exert its influence as a "way of happening":

> it survives
> In the valley of its making where executives
> Would never want to tamper; flows on south
> From ranches of isolation and the busy griefs,
> Raw towns that we believe and die in; it survives,
> A way of happening, a mouth.

Perhaps so. I surely like to think so. I fear, however, that this is not satisfactory as an explanation of the value of a liberal education. It is not, in fact, easy to explain or to describe precisely what it is that a liberal education offers. I think we have to see it in very broad terms—see it, as Arnold wanted us to see life, steadily and whole. It is an education leading to a sweet reasonableness, a state of disinterestedness that enables us to stand outside ourselves and to see ourselves in a light that is not darkness. An education leading to what Arnold called a "spontaneity of consciousness" that works in conjunction with, not in opposition to, a "strictness of conscience." A spontaneity of consciousness that is above all a state of mind leading to a *way* of happening, a mouth, directing us toward workable solutions within the context of reasonable alternatives.

Perhaps, then, the strongest argument for a liberal education is simply that in a free society, where policy is ultimately, if oh so slowly, decided by the public, our decisions will inevitably be no wiser, no richer, no better informed than are our capacities to understand those issues through an awareness of the broader context that a liberal education ideally provides. And while we may temporarily have forgotten to remember—the expensive delicate ship has somewhere to get to and sails calmly on—this is still for many of us the essence of higher education: recovering the past as a means of discovering and shaping the future.

The irony, however, is that, give or take a few adjectives, this is pretty much what every American college and university professes, if not for its entire undergraduate curriculum, at least as regards the role of its general education requirements. What, then, is the difficulty? Why the need to revise, to reexamine, to recommit? Why is the boy falling out of the sky? Viewing education nationally, and considering all levels of higher education, I see a number of reasons. Focusing specifically on problems within large universities, especially those in which research is emphasized, I should like to mention just four.

First, although we in higher education have in the past two decades been obsessed with the ebb and flow of student enrollments, beginning with the campus population explosions of the 1960s, we have not solved the problems inherent in a far more important development—the knowledge explosion. The proliferation of new courses, new majors, new disciplines, and new "interdisciplines" has led colleges and universities to offer a bewildering array of a thousand or more undergraduate courses. The very *substance* of higher education is now confused and confusing—a situation of immense importance to which I will devote my next chapter. But what it comes down to is this: How can we possibly capture and contain knowledge when knowledge will not sit still, when we are forced to divide, even into a thousand parts, in order to conquer?

Second, the power and the glory of a college or university are in its faculty, and the most distinguished institutions are distinguished precisely because of the quality of the men and women they have been able to recruit and retain on their professorial staffs. In most universities today, the large public as well as the elite private institutions, these men and women are, however, first and foremost research scholars, as creative as they are specialized in their work. And although it has been my experience that as a group such scholars take their teaching seriously, they are at their best when teaching advanced students who have the background necessary for exploring with them new areas of knowledge. Not infrequently, they are at their worst when attempting to engage beginning students in those broad-based courses that are the essential starting point for a liberal education. I will have more to say on this subject in later chapters, but we are naive, and our students are misled, if we fail to recognize that the faculty of a first-rate university is different in kind, not quality, from that of a first-rate liberal arts college. We want the best of both worlds in both kinds of institutions, but we must recognize that we do not get it all of the time in all of our faculty.

Third, unlike many of the smaller liberal arts colleges—the Oberlins and Occidentals—today's large universities attempt to accommodate a diverse undergraduate student body that lacks a common background. A liberal education, whatever else it involves, demands a considerable degree of coherence and continuity. To provide such an education to millions of undergraduates, 90 percent of whom have in their high schools majored in fragmentation, is an immensely difficult task. Morever, undergraduates in today's colleges and universities are frequently transients, attaining their education not through sustained study in time and place but through the accumulation, over time and space, of credits. Within crude categorizations, the degree merely attests to the accumulation of an arbitrary number of points—120 semester units, 180 quarter units, congratulations. The very process is antithetical to the idea of seeing it steadily and seeing it whole.

Fourth, finally, and perhaps most importantly, I fear that with all of the talk about the value of the general education requirement, most colleges and universities have failed to agree upon, or even to have spent much time discussing, what precisely they hope to accomplish by imposing it. With a few notable exceptions—Brooklyn College, for instance—most institutions tamper endlessly with their breadth requirements, torture the idea of a core curriculum, but without identifying or defining the outcome. That definition is sorely needed. What is the mark of someone to whom a college or university with any pretensions to excellence awards a bachelor's degree? Or, put another way, what is the least a college or university should expect its undergraduates to attain in the way of knowledge and analytic skills? If that question were answered—and the answer were believed—the rest, I suspect, would be relatively easy.

What might one reasonably expect? Given the way of our world, perhaps not as much as we might like, but I would propose the following as a minimum for ensuring that undergraduates receive a meaningful general education.

1. I think that we should expect students to have the ability to read, to write, and to converse in the English language, and to do so at a level that will enable them to deal effectively with the kind of academic discourse that one expects to find in any institution with serious pretensions to offering a "higher" education.
2. I think that anyone who graduates from a college or university should also have the ability to read and converse in at least one language other than English, and to understand in general how language "works."
3. I believe that graduates should have a basic understanding of the studio and performing arts—origins, historical development, theory, the "artistic sensibility."
4. I think that there should be a similar understanding of the world of letters, and enough background in literary criticism to enable one to read literature, including major works in the fields of philosophy, religion, and the less arcane social sciences, with sensitivity.
5. I think that students should be fully aware of the historical development of humanity—roots, traditions, major shifts in civilization—both East and West.
6. I think that there should be more than a superficial awareness of the physical sciences—the space that surrounds us, the world in which we live—and a solid grasp of the scientific approach to knowledge, especially an understanding of mathematical science.
7. Finally, I think that students should have a similar understanding of our "inner space"—the human body, the workings of the human mind.

One can, of course, argue for other goals and different priorities, an excellent example being the "minimum required curriculum" proposed in *Integrity in the College Curriculum* (Association of American Colleges, 1985, pp. 15–26; see also Koerner, 1981). But my point is that not until such goals are identified and agreed upon can we talk intelligently about required courses and general education programs. There is currently a national obsession with the question of the canon, heated debate as to what texts should and should not be required in the college curriculum. Selectivity for the purpose of classroom presentation is inevitable and will of course always be subject to debate. The important question is really not who or what should be excluded or included (is it to be Homer or Hurston? Dante or Douglass?). What is important is continuity and sequence. To see it steadily, however we define "it," is possible. To see it whole is an impossible dream, and I for one am willing to sacrifice a bit of the whole for coherence.

What I am arguing is that the general education requirements must be approached in terms of "why" and, only very broadly, in terms of "what" (the English Renaissance, yes; Shakespeare, surely; *Hamlet* or *Lear,* what difference does it make?). If we would do this, the "how" could come easily. I have argued in my first chapter that we lack an idea of an education. More specifically, in our colleges and universities we lack a firm idea of a general education, and lacking that we of course lack a liberal education.

Over the past decade or so, my colleagues and I at UCLA have devoted considerable time and effort to "fixing" our own general education requirements, thereby ensuring that our graduates will have "breadth." That we have been less than successful in so doing was revealed in a recent campus survey in which only 7 percent of our fine arts majors claimed to have made substantial progress in understanding the nature of science, only 11 percent in understanding new scientific or technological developments. Similarly, only 14 percent of our engineering majors claimed to have made substantial progress in understanding art, music, and drama, and only 7 percent noted progress in their acquaintance with literature. No matter how long and hard we have struggled to develop meaningful breadth requirements, it is still possible for a student to satisfy them at UCLA without taking a single course carrying the prefix "Philosophy" or, if not that, "History," or "Chemistry," or "Physics," or "Biology," or "Art," or "English," or "Music." This means that it is possible for a student to receive a baccalaureate degree at UCLA without having read a single Greek philosopher, a single Renaissance dramatist, a single American novelist, without having even the most rudimentary knowledge of genetic engineering, DNA, or black holes, without an awareness of the achievement of a Beethoven or a Picasso, an Einstein or a Freud. It means, in short, that our general education requirements do *not* ensure, or even come close to ensuring, that undergraduates receive what the regents of the university long ago mandated—"a broad general education, emphasizing humanistic values and including the required study of science, technology, social sciences, the arts and humanities."

Nor is this situation peculiar to my campus. I noted with dismay recent figures revealing that in 1988–89 a student could earn a bachelor's degree from 37 percent of America's colleges and universities without taking a single course in a history department, could graduate from 45 percent of our colleges and universities without taking a course in American or English literature, from 62 percent without taking a course in philosophy, and from 77 percent without studying a foreign language (Cheney, 1988, p. 5).

To recognize the problem is one thing. To solve it quite another, for the faculties of most colleges and universities have an extraordinary capacity to resist change. Faculties love to play with problems at the margin, pretending that they have made substantive changes while in truth they have made only minor cosmetic adjustments. As William Bowen recognized in one of his reports as president of Princeton University, "There has always been argument over what ought to be included and what can be excluded from a liberal arts curriculum, and the surest way to guarantee a long, disputa-

tious, unsettled and unsettling faculty meeting is to bring to
the floor *any* proposal for a change in the nature or content
of the requirements governing the undergraduate program"
(Koerner, 1981, p. *vi*).

There are many reasons for the reluctance to undertake
a serious reappraisal of general education requirements, most
of them having to do with the self-interests of departments
that are perfectly willing to see changes occur in all areas of
the campus except their own. Because most campuses offer
students the opportunity to satisfy the requirement by choos-
ing from a (usually long) list of courses grouped within
categories and sanctified through tradition, departments,
and especially those individuals who have long taught such
courses, do not want to lose them—which means they do
not want to lose the captive enrollments that come with
them and that help maintain their departmental allocations
of faculty positions and support funds.

In making whatever changes are made, then, the decisions tend to involve merely the addition or deletion of
courses from the general education list. Rather than determining in advance precisely what knowledge and skills the
institution believes its students should acquire and then estab-
lishing courses of study that would ensure that they acquire
them, faculty and administrators shuffle or revise or give new
titles to existing courses to convey the impression that they
will achieve a goal that (usually) has not been defined in the
first place. The attitude seems to be that students can earn
their degrees by taking thirty or forty or fifty courses of almost
any kind and if, on graduating, they are somewhat lopsided—
some unaware of the existence of entire disciplines—well, so
be it. The Great Books are on the shelf, David Attenborough
is on the tube, and there is a Berlitz in every bush.

Is there a better way? I think so, and for a number of
years I advocated one to my colleagues at UCLA. What I
proposed was simply that during their first two years all
undergraduates, regardless of their major interests, should
be required to take the same general education courses. I
advocated eliminating entirely all general education lists and

replacing them with three and only three sequences—one dealing with science and technology, one with the social sciences, and one with the arts and humanities. Each would be a two-year sequence, although I also felt it might be desirable to offer sections in each sequence at a more intense level of instruction so as to accommodate students whose background and interests are in that particular area. There would, for example, be a sequence titled "Science and Technology for Majors" in which students who intend to pursue their upper-division studies in some field of science would enroll, whereas students whose background and interests are in the arts and humanities would presumably take the sequence titled "Science and Technology for Non-Majors." Under such an arrangement, a student might be required to take at least one of the three sequences at the more sophisticated "major" level, although students with an outstanding high school background might choose to take two or all three sequences as potential "majors."

It was, moreover, an essential part of my proposal that each sequence be created anew with our wisest faculty members asked to define what today's students should learn in each of the three areas and then create course sequences that would ensure that they do in fact acquire the desired knowledge and skills. To avoid superficiality and guarantee that goals would be met, I proposed that each sequence be closely overseen by an appropriate campuswide committee, with lectures given only by those faculty members who enjoy and excel at teaching introductory courses to undergraduates. Because at a school as large as UCLA there would inevitably be thousands of students enrolled in each course at the same time, I proposed that to balance breadth with depth, weekly discussion sections taught by lecturers or graduate teaching assistants would be added to offer "in-depth" examination of specific topics. For example, were the sequence in the arts and humanities to be approached chronologically, as well it might, the first course in the sequence would no doubt include a study of ancient Greece and Rome as well as early East Asian and Middle Eastern cultures. During that part of the course devoted to Greece and Rome, some discussion sections might concentrate on the Greek dramatists, others on the Greek and Roman philosophers, others on art and architecture of the period, and still others on the *Iliad* and the *Odyssey*, with the scheduling of such sections undertaken with an eye to matching student and instructor interests.

In such courses, what are now largely separate disciplines would be merged. In the sequence devoted to science and technology, students would see and understand the increasingly close relationships between the physical and life sciences and the ways in which basic science transforms technology. In the social science sequence, students would view a particular issue from a variety of perspectives, seeing how the same problem is approached by a sociologist, an economist, a psychologist, an anthropologist, and so on. And in the arts and humanities sequence, were it to be approached chronologically, students would connect the prose with the passion by viewing a particular period—whether as brief as the French Revolution or as prolonged as the Ming dynasty—not merely from a historical perspective but through its various philosophical and religious beliefs and through its literature, art, and music.

Colleges and universities move with glacial speed, and thus for reasons I have suggested above and will explore more fully in my final chapter, my proposal—which to the outsider may hardly seem to be radical—was far too revolutionary to be taken seriously by my colleagues. Although I initially presented it at a conference intended to explore ways for improving the quality of undergraduate education, the proposal was not even deemed worthy of discussion. Later, perhaps. I take consolation in the hope that later may soon be sooner, and in realizing that there are other institutions currently offering, or at least proposing to offer, programs similar to mine. At the University of Washington, for example, students now have the option of enrolling in a new "college studies" program that links courses in the arts and humanities, the social sciences, and the natural sciences in an attempt to show students how scholars think and how truths change in the various fields. At the University of Kentucky, a "university studies" program requires that students master basic mathematic, communication, and foreign-language skills, and includes courses designed to introduce students to major fields of knowledge and to show how different fields are interrelated. And Hartwick College has a redesigned core program in which students are required to take courses relating to different themes, such as Western civilization, social and global interdependence, and science and technology (Heller, 1988d).

These are, however, exceptions. The vast majority of colleges and universities persist in the pick-and-choose, hit-and-miss approach to a general education, and in so doing they make a travesty of breadth. When I entered college in the mid 1940s as one whose interests, no matter how vaguely defined, were in the arts and humanities, to satisfy my "general education" in the sciences I had the choice of rocks or frogs. I took frogs (my wife was a rock person), and thus while I learned and, remarkably, retained something about the life sciences, my knowledge of the rest of science is considerably less than adequate. I recall complaining to David Saxon when he was president of the University of California that, thanks to a dismal undergraduate education, I had no idea how a light bulb works. He told me that it is quite simple: you just screw it in. At the time I thought that was an unsatisfactory answer, but the more I have considered it, I have come to believe that the answer to providing undergraduate students with a meaningful general education is to do just that. Screw them into a sequence of required courses, one that includes in a logical and coherent presentation the most important things one should know about the world we have inherited and in which we now live.

In the past few years, returning to undergraduate teaching and spending many hours talking to students about their frustrations, frequently their bewilderment, with their majors, I have broadened even further my belief in a more generalized, more liberalized, undergraduate curriculum. Today I have reservations about requiring a major at all, at least a major within just one of the traditional disciplines. Far better, I

have come to believe, to have students in their junior and
senior years concentrate their studies broadly within one of
the three divisions—science and technology, social sciences,
or the arts and humanities. Most of the studies in the second
half of a student's undergraduate career should, in any case,
be "in-depth" studies that would further integrate the traditional disciplines by approaching the material from a variety
of perspectives. And were the first two years to be taught
primarily through large lecture classes utilizing relatively few
members of the regular faculty, in the last two years more
faculty would be available to teach smaller classes, some of
which might involve instructors from two or more disciplines. No formula would necessarily fit all institutions, but
this approach or something similar to it—however adapted
or adopted by colleges and universities—would go a long
way toward ensuring that their graduates had gained a realistic understanding of the totality of the universe of knowledge
as we understand it today. They would, moreover, have moved
beyond a "general" education to something at least approaching the ideal of a true "liberal" education. And my guess is
that those students who would then elect to pursue their studies in graduate school would, as a result of such an undergraduate experience, be far better off than are those students
who today take a smattering of courses in a single discipline
interspersed with a number of unrelated—and unconnected—
electives.

However approached, and with whatever difficulties,
providing a meaningful education to today's twelve million
college students is an essential part of the American dream.
As we continue to strive—and probably fail—to fulfill that
dream to our satisfaction, perhaps it is worth remembering
that, like Icarus, we too are reaching for the sun.

ᴥ 3 ᴪ

THE
KNOWLEDGE EXPLOSION

Emerging Crisis
in the Academic Disciplines

And new philosophy calls all in doubt:
The element of fire is quite put out;
The sun is lost, and the earth, and no man's wit
Can well direct him where to look for it.
                                    —John Donne

In spite of the confusion over the purpose of education and a lack of a clear consensus as to the very meaning of the word, there are today few if any colleges and universities that are not raising questions about their general education requirements, about their undergraduate curriculum, and about the canon—which texts should and should not be required reading. Important as such questions are, I believe they have tended to obscure an even more interesting and difficult problem involving the curriculum—one with which colleges and universities, whether they realize it or not, will have to contend in the near future. I am speaking of changes now occurring within the traditional disciplines, changes that I suspect may alter not only the curriculum but the ways in which colleges and universities are organized into departments, divisions, and schools. Although such changes are by no means peculiar to the humanistic disciplines, I want to

reflect on this problem by examining what has happened
during the past two decades within the discipline that I know
best: literary studies.

I first began to realize that strange things were happening when, in 1971 as newly appointed executive director of
the Modern Language Association, I was compelled to worry
about the MLA annual convention, a three-day meeting that
attracts upward of 10,000 members. As is true of most of the
disciplinary professional associations, the MLA has for more
than 100 years organized its conventions around special interest groups. Since each group is concerned with a different
aspect of language or literature, this format enables members
to come together in small groups to read and hear papers and
to discuss ideas with colleagues who share their interests.

In 1971 the MLA's sections and groups, some seventy
in number, had undergone little change since they were last
reorganized in 1921. Categorized primarily by geography and
chronology, the groups closely paralleled the kinds of course
listings one found, and still finds, in most college catalogs—
seventeenth-century French literature, eighteenth-century German literature, nineteenth-century American literature, twentieth-century Spanish literature, and so on. Beginning in the
late sixties, however, members had increasingly expressed
interest in petitioning for smaller and more specialized one-
time sessions on topics that were not being addressed by the
conservative "official" groups. By the early seventies, such
seminars, as they were called, were not only vastly outnum-
bering the established groups but were attracting far more
members to their meetings.

These seminars were a mixed bag, some treating a
member's favorite author, others focusing on a member's current research interest. At the 1972 convention, for example,
there were seminars in "Research with the Ballad Operas
of Henry Fielding," "The Double in Literature," "Angry
Humor in Contemporary American Writing," "Lucifer in
the Mystery Plays," and the infamous "Literature and Menstruation"—which proved to be so popular that it was
repeated in 1973 as "Menstruation and Literature." But of

greater interest and more indicative of things to come were seminars on such topics as "Marxism and Cultural Studies," "Literature and the Philosophy of History," "Film as Literature," "Women Writers Between the Two Wars," "Semantic Theory," "Women in Yiddish Literature," "Lesbians and Literature," "Racism in Literature," "Sociolinguistics and Literature," and "Literature and Philosophy from Merleau-Ponty to Derrida."

By 1971 it was therefore clear to me and to a good many others that at some point during the dawning of the Age of Aquarius changes had occurred both in what literary scholars were doing and what they were doing it with. In an attempt to understand and thus better accommodate those changes, we decided to survey the MLA members to ascertain what they were actually *doing* as teachers and scholars. The results were fascinating and the survey itself not without interest.

Each member was sent a devilishly simple questionnaire to be completed on what one member, who tore it up in disgust, called a "cute little tangerine computer card." Members were asked to list, in their own words, one, two, or three of what they considered their main scholarly interests and then assign to each interest one or more of thirty-seven general descriptors that would broadly characterize the nature and scope of that interest. The survey evoked an extraordinary number of outraged replies from the membership, partly because it was a computer survey and largely, I have always suspected, because most members had never given much thought to how they approached literary studies and, were they to be perfectly honest, did not really know what they were doing.

One member wrote to tell me that "this is an appalling anti-humanistic idea"; another said, "My innate distrust of machines flares at the sight of this card"; and yet another said, "I cannot cooperate with your survey for I am a sworn enemy of the computer." Those were mild rebukes compared to that of the member who wrote that "my initial bafflement and rage do not abate with time; rather, they intensify to the point of real fury" and concluded his letter with "I won't fill it in! Factor 1, Factor 2, for Christ's sake! I am convinced the MLA has sunk into the quagmire of technological obfuscation!"

In spite of such letters, 70 percent of the members dutifully completed and returned their cute little tangerine cards, from which we compiled a data base of some 42,000 scholarly interests that we then coded into more than 900 descriptors and could have correlated (but did not) in over a million different ways. And what we discovered was precisely what we had suspected: that there was little relationship between what members were actually doing in their scholarly research and writing and the ways in which the MLA and, of far greater significance, the college curriculum were organized to accommodate those interests.

Although in the reorganization that resulted from the survey many of the old geographical-chronological groups were retained, included in the sixty-four new divisions, as they were renamed, were African Literatures, Asian Literatures, Women's Studies in Language and Literature, Ethnic Studies in Language and Literature, Comparative Studies (five separate divisions covering the medieval period to the twentieth century), Popular Culture, Literary Criticism, new genre divisions that included Film, and six separate divisions for various "Approaches to Literature" (Anthropological, Linguistic, Philosophical, Psychological, Religious, and Sociological). Subsequent to that 1973 reorganization, division status has been accorded to Gay Studies in Language and Literature and to Black American Literature and Culture, while discussion groups ("official" units for areas of continuing but more specialized interest) have been added in American Indian Literatures, Asian-American Literature, Chicano Literature, Jewish-American Literature, and Interdisciplinary Approaches to Culture and Society, to mention just a few of those that were not even considered for official status in 1973. Obviously, the field of literary studies was assuming some new and very different directions.

How new and how different none of us involved in the reorganization realized. Perhaps there were too many trees and not enough forest. I had recognized by the end of the sixties, when humanities departments were no longer fearing but finally admitting that the era of expansion was at an end, that the panacea for declining enrollments and disappearing majors had in many departments seemed to rest in the development of interdisciplinary courses and programs. With a hungry eye toward the increased and, so it seemed at the time, ever-increasing student interest in the social sciences, many departments felt that it was at least expedient, if not entirely sensible, to become "relevant" by offering a series of "Literature and . . ." courses. In theory, this was an interesting attempt to provide a broader context for the study of literature by taking it out of the confines of pure esthetics and formal criticism and centering it on those aspects that I believe Matthew Arnold had in mind when he claimed that literature is above all a criticism of life. In practice, however, most such courses were little more than a superficial flirtation between two disciplines—a little of this, a little of that. Most such courses were, in any case, short-lived and did little to restore enrollments to prerevolution levels, because it soon became obvious that what had seemed initially to be student disenchantment with the non-action-oriented humanities was student antipathy toward all the liberal arts and sciences and a turning toward career-oriented professional training.

At the time of the reorganization I was also aware that, by the late sixties, considerable interest had begun to be expressed by virtually all humanities departments in the development of women's and ethnic studies programs, with new courses being added in Afro-American, Latino, Asian, and Native American culture and experience as well as various aspects of women's studies. I do not know how many such courses or programs were initiated in the late sixties—I suspect that in total the course offerings in English departments alone numbered into the thousands—but in any case the MLA convention soon reflected this development by including programs on such topics as "Women and Language," "The Literature of the Chicana," "Contemporary

Native American Literature," "Folklore as Process in Afro-American Literature," and "Asian-American Literature: The Oral Tradition as Literary Style."

That all of these developments, on campuses as well as at the MLA convention, were viewed with dismay by some of the more conservative members of the profession was no doubt inevitable. W. Jackson Bate, writing in 1982, felt that "the progressive trivialization of topics" had made the MLA convention "a laughingstock in the national press" (p. 52). This was quite true. *Ms.* magazine, for instance, had great fun reporting on the "Literature and Menstruation" seminar in an article titled "Out, Damned Spot," and one reporter, after studying the hundreds of sessions available at the 1973 convention, felt that "what made it so hard to decide which session to attend was that there was a strong reluctance to attend any at all." In fairness, however, I should also note that MLA conventions had long been a source of amusement for the press, the author of a 1962 article in the *Washington Post*, for example, having had a hilarious time with topics such as "Acoustic and Orthographic Correlates of the English Syllable Nuclei" or "The Swiss German Hiatus Diphthongization Viewed Structurally," both highly respectable topics which, I suspect, some might also consider to be trivial.

I do not, in any case, intend to linger over these anguished longings for a return to Camelot, to a kind of coherent scholarly exchange that probably never existed either in our colleges and universities or in meetings of the disciplinary associations. Nor do I intend to explore the many factors that by the eighties had led Bate, and many others, to conclude that not just English but all of the humanistic disciplines were "plunging into their worst state of crisis since the modern university was formed a century ago" (p. 46). Others—I note especially Richard Lanham's critique in his brilliant essay on "The 'Q' Question" (1988)—have more than adequately covered this ground, which has, one can only hope, reached its apex in Allan Bloom's myopic effort to open the American mind. If Humpty has indeed fallen, it seems unlikely that Bate, Bennett, Bloom, Booth, or Balch—

who heads a recently formed National Association of Scholars dedicated to "reclaiming the academy"—will ever put Humpty together again.

But to return to my story. In spite of all our coding and correlating, I had completely failed to grasp what was really happening. The survey of MLA membership interests should have told me that something far more basic was occurring than merely the addition of new courses in ethnic or women's studies, or courses that approached literature through themes ("Man and His Myths") or that linked several disciplines ("Literature and Philosophy"). What I missed, and should have realized from the membership survey, was the extent to which literary texts were beginning to be approached in fundamentally different ways through use of not just the texts but also the techniques and language, the mindset, of disciplines such as anthropology, philosophy, linguistics, sociology, and psychology. I was seeing centaurs instead of houyhnhnms and thus did not recognize the inevitability of psychoanalytic and feminist and Marxist criticism, of structuralism and poststructuralism, of semiotics and deconstruction and the new historicism, of what in his 1987 address as MLA president J. Hillis Miller has called the "triumph of theory." Nor could I have foreseen that within two decades undergraduate students at Brown University would be studying semiotics in a "Center for Modern Culture and Media," that students at the University of Illinois at Chicago would be able to fulfill a general education requirement with a course in hermeneutics, that the English department at Syracuse University would be proposing to change its name to "English and Textual Studies," or that Carnegie Mellon's English department would be proudly offering "the nation's first poststructuralist undergraduate curriculum" (Heller, 1988c).

I also missed something else, but this I could not have recognized until I had returned to UCLA as vice-chancellor. With oversight of the academic mission of an entire university, I began to realize the extent to which not just literary and humanistic disciplines but virtually all of the traditional disciplines were experiencing fundamental change. Whether these changes are for the better or for the worse is irrelevant. They are real and, given the expansion of knowledge and the increasing dependency of one field upon another, they are here to stay. Interdisciplinary programs will continue to develop, and the traditional disciplines will become increasingly difficult to define, will become, as many already are, "blurred genres," to use Clifford Geertz's happy phrase. My concern, then—and today it is perhaps my greatest concern about the future of higher education—is not that these things are happening but that they are happening without a semblance of a plan and even, I suspect, without many campuses realizing that they are happening.

It is not difficult to document such changes. For example, as is true in most universities today, on my campus it has become increasingly difficult to differentiate between many of the science departments that have traditionally been categorized within either a life science or a physical science division. At UCLA a background in mathematics, physics, and chemistry is now necessary for a baccalaureate degree in biology, while students majoring in biochemistry are required or permitted to take as many courses in biology or microbiology as they are in chemistry. Molecular biology is not studied in a department at all, although we have a Molecular Biology Institute and an interdepartmental graduate degree program that draws upon work being done in at least five separate departments, including several in the School of Medicine. Arnold Thackray, director of the Center for the History of Chemistry, claims, and it would seem correctly, that "the world of our experience does not come to us in the pieces we have been carving out" (Winkler, 1987, p. A14). Indeed, one is forced to question whether there continue to be any meaningful distinctions between the biological and the physical sciences, as practiced and taught today.

This situation is by no means peculiar to the sciences. Robert Scholes, director of the Center for Modern Culture and Media at Brown University, now suspects that "the humanities and some of the social sciences are shrinking into one large discipline" (Winkler, 1987, p. A15). History, for instance, is a social science on some campuses, my own included, while on many others (and by the National Endowment for the Humanities) it is considered to be a humanistic discipline. At UCLA anthropology is classed as a social science, but with roots in both the biological sciences and humanistic studies and with strong ties to other disciplines ranging from anatomy and genetics to linguistics, classics, and fine arts. Psychology is considered to be a "biosocial" science and is located in a division for life sciences; only a concentration in psychobiology leads to a bachelor of science degree, however, while other concentrations, including the increasingly popular cognitive science (which requires chemistry, mathematics, physics, and computer courses), lead to a bachelor of arts degree. Some twenty years ago the study of linguistics was included in UCLA's Department of English, and although Linguistics is now a separate department it continues to reside in the division for the humanities—and this in spite of the fact that the discipline now includes such subjects as disorders of language development, linguistic anthropology, computational linguistics, neurolinguistics, psycholinguistics, and sociolinguistics.

A few years ago, for my own amusement and the possible edification of my colleagues, I listed ten undergraduate courses I had selected from the UCLA catalog and asked colleagues to tell me in which department they thought these ten courses were offered. The average number of correct answers was three. "Urban and Regional Planning and Development" turns out to be a political science course, "Third World Political Thought" is taught in the philosophy department, "Perspectives in the Study of American Culture" is an English course, "Origins and Histories of Crop Plants" is a geography course, and "Nonrenewable Resources and Society" appears in the catalog under "Earth and Space Sciences."

Further indication of this blurring of disciplines can be found in the plethora of new interdisciplinary centers and institutes that in recent years have sprung up on virtually every campus in the country. Such institutes have long existed in the sciences and social sciences, although not to the extent that they exist at present (and promise to expand in the future under current policies of the National Science Foundation and other federal agencies). But in the past decade the humanities have been getting into the act. In addition to the National Humanities Center, a privately funded think tank in North Carolina, it is estimated that there are today as many as 300 humanities centers or institutes on America's college and university campuses. Murray Krieger, founding director of the University of California's new Humanities Research Institute, explains this phenomenon: "There's a tremendous underground rumbling all around the university about the structure of humanistic education. Centers are the creative way to do the humanities these days" (Heller, 1988b, p. A4).

Occasionally called "hidden universities," these centers and institutes might more accurately be termed "hidden departments" or "hybrid departments." Although most offer no courses and have no faculty positions of their own, for many scholars they have become a home away from home, away from their single-discipline departments. Those self-contained towers we call departments, and into which we assumed we had gathered specialists with closely shared interests, we now find have large cracks through which hands are reaching out in all directions, grasping at someone else's specialty, shaking the towers to their very foundations. One recognizes that such relationships, such mergers, have in the past created "interdisciplines" that over time have become new disciplines replacing the old. What we are dealing with here, however, are not isolated instances but virtually the entire realm of knowledge, the very substance of higher education. As Steven Muller has noted, "Knowledge is increasingly fragmented" and the university "is losing its intellectual coherence, its disciplinary coherence"; it "has splintered and fragmented in every way" (Hayes, 1986, p. 70). No one, I suspect, has seen this as clearly as has Clifford Geertz. Recognizing that the "present jumbling of varieties of discourse" has made it difficult even to label authors or to classify works, Geertz concludes that

it is more than a matter of odd sports and occasional
curiosities, or of the admitted fact that the innovative
is, by definition, hard to categorize. It is a phenomenon general enough and distinctive enough to suggest
that what we are seeing is not just another redrawing
of the cultural map—the moving of a few disputed
borders, the marking of some more picturesque moun-
tain lakes—but an alteration of the principles of map-
ping. Something is happening to the way we think
about the way we think [1983, p. 20].

But here's the rub. While disciplines and "interdisciplines" are amorphous, are not academic units, departments
are. And departments have a life of their own—insular,
defensive, self-governing, compelled to protect their interests
because the faculty positions as well as the courses that justify
funding those positions are located therein. A department is
therefore constantly in competition with other departments
and in dubious battle with the administration for maintaining, if not increasing, their support funds and the number
of their faculty positions. All faculty members belong to a
department and thus even those who today have little or no
concern with what the department has traditionally represented are forced to defend and support it because the department, not the discipline, is the hand that feeds.

Moreover, because tenured faculty have what are in
effect lifetime contracts, within departments the old guard
have increasingly become at odds with what I (and John
Donne) have called the "new philosophies," not only because
the old guard are frequently unsympathetic to what are
viewed as fads (this is especially true in the humanistic and
social science disciplines), but because, having devoted their
careers to a particular kind of study, upon retirement they
want to see their position filled by someone who will continue to do whatever it was they had been doing—a perverse
if understandable form of academic immortality.

One sees this conflict in all departments, although in
the sciences the blurring of disciplines has become so com-

mon that change is accommodated with relative ease. At many universities zoology and botany have easily been subsumed in biology, and, to create a new discipline (if not necessarily a new department) in the physical sciences, one need merely add the prefix *bio* to the old—biochemistry, biophysics, biomathematics, biostatistics. Moreover, because in the sciences "discovery" occurs wherever today's action is, those faculty members who are unwilling or unable to adjust their research from yesterday's action to today's are seldom troublesome. They teach undergraduates or become administrators. But in the humanities and some of the social sciences, where the old order seldom changes permanently and "truth" is largely a matter of opinion and approach, those who believe that they have discovered new truths through relationships with other disciplines are not infrequently viewed by the old guard (of whatever age) as intent on destroying not just the discipline but the department. Not surprisingly, therefore, as the new philosophers find themselves frustrated at having to teach the traditional courses, forcing their new wine into old bottles, in many of the humanistic disciplines we have for the past decade been seeing fierce internal dissension.

The *Chronicle of Higher Education,* which provides the most extensive coverage of meetings of the disciplinary associations, is the best source for gaining insight into this situation. Glancing through issues published in the 1980s, one finds a philosophy professor claiming that "there's a sectarian frenzy among philosophers today," with philosophers tending to go off into their own corner to pursue their own specialty, "too unaware—and too condemnatory—of what goes on in other corners" (Hook, 1981, p. 3). A distinguished historian accuses his profession of having adapted history to the "pseudo, value-free scholarship" of the social sciences and claims that "we historians have not produced, and are not now producing, a cumulative, credible body of organized knowledge" that could be valuable to society (Winkler, 1981, p. 7). In the field of literature, a lengthy critique of "deconstruction and other critical conditions" begins by describing how "the 'moldy fig academics' have lined up against the 'hermeneutical mafia' in literature departments across the country. The moldy figs think the mafia has produced a lot of 'overblown moonshine.' The mafia thinks the moldy figs are nothing but 'handmaidens' of literature" (Coughlin, 1982, p. 27). And in reviewing the current state of all of the humanistic disciplines, a recent article succinctly summarizes the debate by asking, "Is study of the humanities too specialized, too insulated, too politicized, and too professionalized? Or is this a moment of intellectual ferment, increasing student interest, and true scholarly democracy?" (Heller, 1988a, p. A11). The answer to all these questions—and herein lies the problem—would seem to be yes. For even if we make allowance for reportorial exuberance and recognize that new directions in scholarship have always been cause for legitimate debate, anyone who has attended recent meetings of professional associations in the humanities or has had occasion to dabble in their scholarly journals must suspect that the current dissension is different from past debates, questioning as it does not merely the direction and content but the value of entire disciplines.

Putting aside internal dissension, what is clear from all this, or at least clear to me, is that while what we study and teach in colleges and universities has changed dramatically in the past few decades—for better or for worse—and promises to continue to do so in the next few, how we organize ourselves to study and teach it has not. As long as we continue to compromise what we know to be in the best interests of research and teaching, continue to operate within academic units—schools, divisions, departments—devised to accommodate academic programs many years out of date, we will be offering inadequate training for those students who are going to be the faculty members of the next century and, as regards my main concern in this book, will be further confusing an already confused undergraduate curriculum. Standing in line, shaking hands with some 3,000 of UCLA's entering freshmen a few years ago, I noted that the vast majority, those with the brightest eyes and the bushiest tails, were "undeclared." Those are the ones who, I suspect, have looked closely at our catalog, have studied the confusing mass of a hundred or more majors leading to a baccalaureate degree, the thousands of courses offered in some fifty departments, and have simply thrown up their hands in despair, unable to select any one of the above.

But what disturbs me most about all this is that even among those who share my belief in the reality if not necessarily the importance of these changes, there is no serious effort to alter or even to question the way their colleges and universities are presently organized into schools, divisions, and departments. There have been some modest attempts (at Berkeley, at the University of Chicago, and perhaps most notably at Brooklyn College) to engage in a rethinking of the academic organization, but such efforts are few and far too limited in scope. What we need is a major national analysis— a membership survey, if you will—of what is really happening with scholarship and teaching in today's colleges and universities and of what we can reasonably assume will occur in the next quarter-century. In light of what such an analysis reveals, we then need to take a hard look at the academic structure of our institutions and reconsider the ways in which our units and programs are organized.

It may be that we will have to rethink what we mean by a degree program and begin to describe our interests and our work in radically different terms, as Richard Lanham has proposed in *Literacy and the Survival of Humanism* (1983). In so doing, we may bring not just the undergraduate curriculum but the very idea of an undergraduate major into question. There is surely nothing wrong with students in the junior and senior years electing to concentrate their studies in a particular area, but there is also much to be said (and in the previous chapter I have tried to say it) for students ranging over a number of closely related fields in their advanced studies. I believe that the institution has an obligation to accommodate both extremes while still imposing a reasonable degree of order and coherence on its undergraduate offerings and ensuring that its program reflects current knowledge and thinking. At present the undergraduate curriculum has been compromised to the extent that it is incoherent. One of the main reasons that efforts to provide a satisfactory liberal education are being frustrated is that the very *substance* of higher education can no longer be adequately accommodated through the traditional departments, disciplines, courses, and undergraduate majors.

It may be that departments as we know them today are no longer viable, that we need larger or at least different kinds of units that can encompass more than a single field, however broadly redefined, and in which degree programs can flourish without students or faculty having to show their passports when moving from one area to another. The way disciplines presently are and long have been divided into departments is arbitrary. Why, for instance, should the study of literature be spread across ten or more departments while the study of history is generally encompassed in one? In foreign-language departments, why is the literature of a particular country but not its history or philosophy or art normally taught? Why, if we choose to divide the cake geographically, do we not have a department of "France" or of "China"? Why not study the past in comprehensive chronological units with departments of "The Nineteenth Century" or "Nineteenth-Century Europe" or "Nineteenth-Century America" rather than separating scholars (and courses) concerned with those periods into a dozen or more departments? Or are such chronological-geographical divisions still viable at all?

What we presently do is indeed arbitrary, but it is also deeply embedded in tradition. The traditionalist will therefore argue that, in dividing the substance of higher education into what for classroom purposes are digestible units, one plan is no better than another. Perhaps so, but this is true only so long as the plan does not distort what we know to be reality, does not deny a student the opportunity to see it, whatever "it" might be, in its entirety, does not deter access to whatever perspective one seeks. Today, in many areas on a campus, that is precisely what is happening.

There is no simple solution to this problem. I see no
easy way to resolve the inconsistencies between what we teach
and what we increasingly realize should be taught, or to
resolve the conflict between what scholar-teachers currently
do and the ways in which colleges and universities are organized to enable them to do it. Jaroslav Pelikan has made the
interesting suggestion that what he calls the "three modalities
of university education—undergraduate, graduate, and professional"—might be related to one another "on a divisional
basis, through faculty appointments and through programs
of instruction and research, with each professional school
related symbiotically to one (or more) of the divisions" (1983,
p. 47). That might be a partial answer for those large research
universities that involve these three "modalities," but it would
not address problems within institutions that do not have
graduate or professional programs, nor would it solve the
problems I have described within the various humanistic
disciplines.

The question that each institution must ultimately ask
itself in looking at its academic programs and administrative
structures is whether the form appropriately follows the function. Regrettably, the curriculum of most colleges and universities today has to be deemed formless, for as I have tried to
show in previous chapters, we have no clear idea of an education and consequently no clear idea of the function. The sun
is lost, and no man's wit can well direct him where to look
for it. But surely, undergraduate education aside, at least in
an institution whose mission includes basic research that
involves discoveries of importance to all humankind, it is
essential that the form, the administrative structure, not be
an obstacle to the academic pursuit. At present I fear that it
is, or is rapidly so becoming.

I have no illusions that change will be easy, and I am
certain that by most it will be unwelcome. I am also certain,
however, that what we fail to do today in considering this
issue will haunt us tomorrow, for as long as we continue to
compromise between what we know, on the one hand, and

what we teach, on the other, as long as we continue to train within outmoded structures those students who are tomorrow's faculty, we will retain those structures, with all their limitations and inconsistencies. And, as a result, we will continue to make a mess of the undergraduate curriculum and of a liberal education.

❦ 4 ❧

READING
AND WRITING

Essentials for a
Coherent Curriculum.

I gotta use words when I talk to you
But if you understand or if you dont
That's nothing to me and nothing to you
We all gotta do what we gotta do
—T. S. Eliot

As I have suggested in my first chapter, it all begins with communication, which for anyone seriously aspiring to an education in this country means the ability to read and write the English language, and to do so with reasonable skill. Because over the past fifty or so years English departments in most colleges and universities have relinquished their claim to the study and teaching of rhetoric, speech, language, and linguistics, their stock in trade has been reduced to reading and writing—and I do not use the words loosely or in any way to belittle the study of literature. Although many college and university English departments would deny it, would insist that the teaching of literature is one thing—the thing they "do"—while reading and writing are something else, English departments fundamentally deal with communication.

That college and university English departments are frequently paranoid when it comes to differentiating between the teaching of literature and the teaching of reading and writing is something I have never understood. In teaching English courses for some thirty years I have always been under the impression that whether my course is freshman composition or a graduate seminar in Dickens, I am indeed teaching reading and writing. When I teach the Victorian authors, at whatever level, I try to help my students develop sensitivity in reading the works and sophistication in writing about them. In my own writing about the Victorians I attempt to persuade my readers to read a work the way I read it, with the assumption that others will write about what I have written and will in turn help me to be a more sensitive reader. My subject *is* reading and writing. My job as a teacher of literature is to engage a class, whether of freshmen or of Ph.D. candidates, in the totality of a poem or novel or play or essay—its language, its form, its imagery, its meaning, its magic—and to try to make that work come to life for my students as they truly read it, make it happen, perhaps for the first time. That to me is what teaching literature in an English department is all about—making it accessible, making it real, teaching how to read and thus better to understand the most sublime and subtle works of literature, whenever and wherever they were written.

When I teach composition, whether in a course labeled "Composition" or in any other course offered by the English department, my greatest challenge—and for me or any composition teacher the greatest reward, because herein lies the greatest opportunity for a student's growth—is at that level of writing where the student is still struggling not with grammar or mechanics but with organizing thought. Grammar and mechanics are arbitrary and far less important than we think they are—which does not prevent otherwise sane individuals from fumbling over their personal pronouns when introduced to a professor of English (as if most of us really cared). Grammar comes with experience, vocabulary with an increased need for subtlety of expression. But the true magic in writing is in the creative process, not just what oft was thought but ne'er so well expressed, but for the student what had never been adequately expressed at all and thus, for that individual (or so I would contend), never really thought at all. It is the thrill—and I know no better word to describe it—of capturing an idea, a thought, an emotion, and knowing that you have adequately conveyed it to another human being through language. It is the power that comes through the ability to command a language so as to describe, to assert, to persuade, to debate—above all, to evaluate, to understand, to know. That is what it is all about, and whether or not a teacher can add to that power a touch of the poet, we are still dealing with the one essential prerequisite for learning, the open-sesame to education and certainly to anything with pretensions to being called "higher" education.

Writing, so defined, makes "Composition" the most important course in the curriculum. It is truly the heart of the matter, and the fact that writing is taught, for the most part, badly, that it is far too often scorned by English professors as a demeaning course assignment, is one of the most depressing comments on English departments today. It will not do to blame the problem on somebody else—the directors of doctoral dissertations who, realizing that their candidates cannot write, wonder whatever happened to undergraduate education; the upper-division instructors who blame the freshman composition program; the composition instructors who damn the high schools; the high school teachers who look back in anger at the elementary schools and the parents. We are beyond the point of blame. We are, as the National Commission on Excellence in Education (1983) reported some seven years ago, quite simply a nation at risk.

My first acquaintance with composition courses was at the University of Wisconsin, where in the fall of 1958 I began working toward my doctorate in English and, as a first-time teaching assistant, was assigned two sections of English 1A with twenty-five students in each. I had taken a similar course some thirteen years earlier as a freshman at the University of Missouri but had no memory of it. In the intervening years I had written a good deal but, like most of my graduate student colleagues, was without training or experience in teaching composition prior to finding myself on the happy side of the lectern. I recall purchasing a paperback on English grammar and frantically trying to memorize the parts of speech before meeting my first class.

Fortunately, for me as well as my students, in those days the year-long composition sequence was taken seriously at Wisconsin and, I assume, at most comparable institutions. My memory is that there were several hundred sections of English 1A and 1B, all carefully supervised by two professors, Ednah Thomas and Edgar Lacy. Meetings with beginning T.A.'s were held weekly, and during that first semester Ednah Thomas managed to visit one of each of our classes, sitting quietly in the rear of the room with an uncanny ability to make herself invisible to everyone except the teaching assistant. Following her visit, we T.A.'s met with Professor Thomas for a postmortem on our class and were asked to submit in advance of this meeting three themes from the previous week's assignment. One theme was to be selected because we deemed it to be outstanding, one because it fell in the medium range, and one because we considered it to be conspicuously weak. Although I now suspect she said it to all the T.A.'s, to this day I can remember Ednah Thomas looking up at me over her glasses (surely she wore glasses?), my carefully selected papers spread on the desk before her, saying something to the effect that the papers were all very interesting, but Mr. Schaefer, which one is supposed to be outstanding?

The students wrote a dozen papers each semester, read a good deal about writing, took some horrendous tests on grammar, and, I suspect, came away from the course at best with improved writing skills, at worst no worse for wear. On the contrary, although the kinds of things we tested in those courses are long out of fashion ("define vulgate level, puristic standards, localism"; "in the appropriate spaces in the following paragraph give the part of speech and the function for each numbered word"), the two-semester sequence was a logical and coherent approach to composition instruction. Jane Austen's *Emma*, Dickens's *Hard Times*, and a number of short stories were required reading in English 1B that year, but the students wrote twelve themes and the emphasis on composition was primary. Those were the days.

Not so the sixties. The sixties were different. As the postwar babies boomed onto the college scene, enrollments on many campuses quickly doubled or even tripled, new campuses seemed to spring up overnight, funds flowed freely, and the hiring of new faculty occurred at an unprecedented rate. When I came to UCLA in 1962, Ph.D. hot in hand, the academic job market was tight, and I was one of four fortunate assistant professors appointed that year. In the mid and late sixties, however, the job market, as it always has and always will, turned around, and between 1965 and 1969, a five-year period, UCLA's English department hired fifty-five new assistant professors (twenty-two of whom, for those who might be curious, still hold what are now tenured positions in the department). It was a wholesale operation, hiring by the dozen. One paid one's money and took one's chances.

In retrospect, it is easy to understand why things got out of control, "hysterical" rather than (as we then thought) "halcyon" being the appropriate adjective for most of those years. And while the headlines focused on the explosive and at times tragic events at Berkeley, Columbia, Wisconsin, and Kent State, what was happening quietly within most (one likes to think not all) colleges and universities—the erosion of academic standards, the loss of certain requirements, the deterioration of teaching—had a more lasting effect on higher education than any of the "revolutions."

My concern here, however, is with the teaching of composition, which, after the smoke had cleared in the seventies, we began to recognize as a crisis. It is now obvious that the problems began in the early sixties with the influx of students. In 1962, my first semester at UCLA, two of my three courses were in composition, one with thirty-five, the other with thirty-seven students, which meant that I had some seventy themes to read and comment on each week while lecturing to fifty students in my third course, a literature survey, and trying to rewrite my dissertation for publication. Although I taught freshman composition five times that first year and—or so I like to think—became reasonably effective in teaching it, after that initiation I was deemed ready to help meet the demand for the "real" courses in literature and thus subsequently taught freshman composition only one more time. The composition courses were sometimes taught by new assistant professors but primarily by teaching assistants and increasingly by a large number of underpaid and vastly over-worked lecturers on one-year appointments—youngish men and women who, because of either geographical confinement or less than stellar academic credentials, could not obtain assistant professorships even in a seller's market. We hired a director of composition and held weekly T.A. instruction sessions similar to those I had encountered at Wisconsin, but the sheer numbers did us in. At UCLA we also got caught up in a national craze: the freshman seminar syndrome, wherein young instructors held sway on everything from T. S. Eliot to the Vietnam War while asking students to write an occasional paper. And how else could it be? By the end of the decade UCLA had some 20,000 enrollments in English each year, and—the University of California having changed from the semester to the quarter system—freshman composition had been reduced to a ten-week course taught by instructors who frequently were as indifferent to the subject as they were unqualified to teach it.

The situation was hardly unique to UCLA. Even as early as 1963 Francis Keppel, the U.S. commissioner of education, warned that the teaching of English was so poor that it had "reached a desperate point that threatens the nation's educational system" (Wehrwein, 1963, p. 23). More-over, by mid-decade the increasing number of ethnic minori-ties—for many of whom college-level English was a second dialect if not a second language—exacerbated an already impossible situation. To further complicate matters, the chil-dren of the sixties waved their magic flowers in an attempt to make all college requirements vanish and, while failing to make a clean sweep, caused at least half of all institutions either to reduce or to eliminate their undergraduate English requirements.

In most institutions the freshman English requirement included an introduction to literature as well as instruction in composition. Had it merely been the literature component that was eliminated, while we in the humanities might have bemoaned the implied lack of standards, we could no doubt have sympathized with, say, science departments that claimed it was at least as important for students to be introduced to science as it was for them to be introduced to literature. What happened, however, was that the composition requirement was frequently phased out with the rest, leaving a generation of college students whose limited writing skills were an accurate reflection of their limited mentalities. There may have been lots of imagination, lots of "soul" in that generation— what we came to call the "grass-ass" generation because of frequent student insistence on holding classes on the lawn— but during those years I saw and heard pathetically little in the way of facility for expressing ideas. What one heard was the sound of the siren and the bull-horn, the sound of breaking glass, the sound of inept slogans being taped to the plywood that had replaced the broken glass. One heard the silent ineloquence of the bumper-sticker. The words, such as they were, tended to be warmed-over Walter Cronkite, monotonously broken by the ubiquitous interjection of "you see" and "you know." I recall listening in amazement to our Academic Senate as it endlessly debated whether a strike was a *strike* or simply a *moratorium,* concluding that it did not really matter what we called it as long as we all felt the same way about it. And as our chancellor, Charles Young, was being interviewed on our giant-screen, closed-circuit television set, I watched in wonder while one excessively hairy young student, shaking defiantly his defiant fist and responding with the wisdom of his ages, shouted at the screen, "Fuck you, Chuck." Those were the years of the verbal orgasm, years when it seemed that the best had lost all conviction and the worst were full of passionate intensity—and very little else.

During the sixties some English departments, aware that the teaching of composition is not only difficult but expensive and time-consuming, simply gave up in despair of ever doing an adequate job. Exhibiting creative imagination of an unusual kind and on an extraordinary scale, they pretended that the high schools had prepared students to read and write at a level that would enable them to pursue what we were still calling higher education and thus proceeded to drop not only the requirement but the course. Many departments, especially those that continued trying to service large numbers of captive freshmen, seemed to feel, as we did for a time at UCLA, that they could do the job more effectively by disguising the subject as a seminar on a contemporary topic— one on which a number of essays were in theory, but not always in practice, to be written. Some departments, recognizing that the graduate student T.A. more frequently needed to take a composition course than to teach one, tried to bring back into the program their experienced senior faculty, but in many instances this was a more unfortunate experience for the students than if they had been taught by a totally inexperienced, largely incompetent, but at least enthusiastic graduate student. And an increasing number of departments seemed more than willing to share the composition requirement with departments of speech or drama—departments that were happy enough to get the increased enrollments. What was needed, of course, for many of those students was not just the traditional composition course but highly specialized programs in remedial work with the kind of teachers that few graduate schools had adequately prepared and even fewer colleges, especially the two-year colleges, could afford to hire. That the three R's of higher education were being viewed as reading, writing, and relevance might possibly have been a healthy development—but not without the reading and writing.

We survived the sixties and the seventies too, although at what cost to higher education we have yet to determine. The sins of the sixties continue to be visited on the eighties. Fortunately, however, by the end of the seventies many institutions, frequently bypassing their English departments, began to take a second look at their writing programs and to introduce some significant changes. Whether what even the most enlightened colleges and universities are now offering their students is making a difference or whether it is still too little and, for most students, too late is unclear. What is clear is that the vast majority of college students continue to be deficient in writing skills.

In *Composition and the Academy: A Study of Writing Program Administration* (1986), Carol Hartzog has analyzed changes that have recently occurred in writing programs at the institutions belonging to the Association of American Universities. These elite fifty or so universities are of particular interest, not merely because of their prestige or the fact that they graduate a high percentage of America's doctorates, but because, given the relatively high quality of the undergraduate students they admit, their recognition of the need for strong writing programs is indicative of the seriousness of the problem. What Hartzog found was that thirty-six of the forty-four institutions responding to her survey acknowledged that within the past ten years their writing programs had undergone major changes, and even the eight that reported no change stated that changes were being planned or that other developments on campus had strengthened their writing programs (p. 4). Interestingly, and supportive of my earlier comments about attitudes toward writing in English departments, it appears that today only half of these universities now center their writing programs solely within English departments, the others either having independent programs (Harvard's "Program in Expository Writing," the "MIT Writing Program") or having taken to administering programs interdepartmentally or directly through deans' offices (at Yale the writing program, advised by an interdisciplinary faculty committee, reports to the dean of Yale College) (pp. 14–15).

A case in point is what happened on my own campus. Although in the late sixties when I chaired UCLA's English department I was, like most of us, not fully aware of the seriousness of the problem, when I returned to the campus as vice-chancellor in 1978 my highest priority was to strengthen UCLA's composition program. Richard Lanham, in *Literacy and the Survival of Humanism* (1983), has described in considerable detail what we attempted and, for the most part, accomplished following his appointment in 1979 as director of the new "UCLA Writing Programs," and I will not repeat his description. Suffice it to say that the success of these programs, which I believe to be as good as any and better than most, can mainly be credited to three factors. First, Lanham, a student of rhetoric and the Renaissance, had for many years been studying and writing about the composition problem and thus had a clear vision of where he wanted to go with a new effort. Second, although the writing programs were technically associated with the English department, they were given semiautonomous status and sufficient independent funding to enable Lanham to surmount the university bureaucracy (and the indifference of most of our colleagues in the English department) and thus move speedily in implementing his ideas. Third, and in some ways most important, in staffing the new programs Lanham determined not to rely primarily on either graduate student teaching assistants or English professors but, through a well-advertised national search, to hire some forty full-time lecturers who had a genuine, proven interest in composition. Moreover, in hiring these lecturers Lanham insisted that they have at least a reasonable prospect of more than a one-year appointment and that their salaries and teaching loads be roughly comparable to those of assistant professors, thereby in large measure avoiding the second-class citizenship that threatens the success of any university initiative not dominated by the professoriat.

I think we all recognize that the schools, for a variety of reasons—many of them beyond their control—have done and are continuing to do a less than adequate job in teaching reading and writing, and there is no need to belabor this point or to document it. The problem has been caused by a failure in educational sequence, from kindergarten through college. But fixing composition programs in the elementary and secondary schools is a long-term process and involves far more than a renewed commitment on the part of colleges and universities to train better teachers (although one must surely applaud the efforts of the National Writing Project, which from its modest beginnings as the Bay Area Writing Project now involves 117 university-based sites in 44 states; Boyer, 1987, p. 79). What most colleges and universities are struggling with is, however, an immediate problem involving students currently in the classroom at whatever level, Ph.D. candidates included; the problem is no longer confined, if it ever was, to entering freshmen. In returning to teaching this year after a seventeen-year hiatus, I suspect that I am able to recognize the problem more readily than colleagues who have lived with the erosion year by year. What I have found are English graduate students writing at a level that should be considered mediocre for a sophomore, senior English majors submitting unrevised papers that reveal writing problems of the kind one expects to encounter in a freshman composition course, and freshmen writing at what I would deem to be an eighth-grade level. Lanham has probably not exaggerated in claiming that "the high school sophomore writing at second-grade level now finds a counterpart in the young lawyer writing like a high school sophomore" (1983, pp. 144–178).

There is indeed a short-term and a long-term problem, and until the latter is successfully addressed we will continue to live with the former. Changes that have occurred in college and university writing programs—a concern with process more than with product, sustained efforts to write "across the curriculum," increasing use of computer-aided instruction, smaller classes and more tutorials, improved methods of testing, the creation of specialized courses to meet special needs or interests, and a host of others—are clearly moving in the right direction. Still, the sheer magnitude of the task, to say nothing of the cost, tends to be overwhelming. In 1987–88 at UCLA we offered 234 sections of composition courses at the lower-division level, 85 sections for upper-division students, and 3 at the graduate level—a total of 322 sections accommodating nearly 7,000 students. Unfortunately, this effort is far from adequate. Had we the funds (and the classrooms and the qualified teachers) to enable us to double the number of sections, we would still, I sadly conclude, have hundreds, perhaps thousands, of students with serious writing problems.

There is no panacea, no single approach to writing instruction that will miraculously solve this problem in the schools or in postsecondary institutions. In addition to an endless flow of "how to" textbooks, in the past quarter-century we have seen numerous books and articles dealing with composition theory and proposing a wide range of different approaches (for example, Kitzhaber, 1963; Shaughnessy, 1977; Lanham, 1979; White, 1985; and Neel, 1988). But whatever the approach—and it is not my purpose in this chapter to summarize much less evaluate the current state of composition theory and practice—to me one of the most troublesome aspects of the composition crisis is the lingering belief in colleges and universities that were education in the schools to be fixed, higher education could get out of the business of teaching writing. Because of this belief, in many institutions the elementary composition courses are still treated as being remedial—courses for which college credit is given, if given at all, grudgingly. The implication is that the students are at fault for having failed to develop the kinds of writing skills that are necessary for pursuing higher education. In many instances this well may be the case, but in the thirty years since I first taught a composition course at Wisconsin, I doubt if I have come across more than a dozen students who could not have profited from demanding college-level courses in composition, not just in their freshman but in their junior or senior years also. That today there are literally millions of entering college students who need an intensive secondary or even elementary school writing course merely confuses the issue and casts an aura of remediation over the entire enterprise.

The higher part of higher education, or so we make it seem, applies to all courses except those involving composition. We treat writing as if it were something one is supposed to master at an early age, like walking, rather than seeing it as a difficult skill that can always be improved and must constantly be pursued if one is serious about advanced studies. Education, I have argued, begins with communication, but that does not mean that the development of communication skills ends in the elementary or secondary schools. "Consider the message that would be sent to the schools and to the society at large," writes Mike Rose, were the university to embrace, not just financially but conceptually, the teaching of writing—"if we gave it full status, championed its rich relationship with inquiry, insisted on the importance of craft and grace, incorporated it into the heart of our curriculum" (1985, p. 359). Until we do that, until we recognize that there is such a thing as advanced composition and that it is not only a legitimate but an essential part of a college degree program, composition courses will continue to be treated as an unfortunate part of the college curriculum. Failing to recognize this, no matter what good things may eventually happen in the schools, our colleges and universities will continue to have a crisis in composition.

*   *   *   *

A postscript. Over the past two decades it has been my good fortune to meet and, in various ways, to work with many of the leading literary scholars and critics of my generation. Among this group there is no one I hold in higher esteem than J. Hillis Miller, with whom I had the opportunity to consult on a wide range of professional issues during my years as executive director of the Modern Language Association. In opening the May 1987 issue of *PMLA,* the association's prestigious journal, I was therefore delighted to come upon the concluding paragraphs of the address Miller had recently delivered as MLA president. "I conclude," Miller wrote, "by saying that our main professional responsibility, at all levels of instruction, remains what it has always been, to teach the basics: reading and the good writing that can only occur if it is accompanied by good reading" (p. 291).

Miller went on, however, to say that "real reading is not just a recognition of the way the rhetorical or tropological dimension of language undermines straightforward grammatical and logical meaning. It is also an attempt, no doubt an impossible attempt, to confront what language itself has always already erased or forgotten, namely, the performative or positional power of language as inscription over what we catachrestically call the material."

After reading these concluding remarks I naturally went back and read the entire address, "The Triumph of Theory, the Resistance to Reading, and the Question of the Material Base." I read it three times, in fact, trying hard to confront the performative power of Miller's language as inscription over what we call, catachrestically or not, the material. And I concluded that this extraordinary essay by one of our most brilliant scholars exemplifies yet another problem that I have increasingly encountered with reading and writing—namely, my difficulty in reading what is currently being written by many of the literary elite in our English departments.

Some years ago I had occasion to go through a number of abstracts of articles that had recently been published in *PMLA:*

> The proponents of modernism, in their putative wish to be free of inherited patterns, release a compensatory reaction, an anxiety over the sense of a lost relationship with tradition. In this context, the critical dogma lamenting the "anxiety of influence" may be seen as one modernist's attempt to regain a relationship with the past at the expense of the equally recalcitrant doctrine of originality.

> By creating a text on two levels, a level of unsuccessful referentiality and a level of language as an autonomous entity, he replaces the notion of a vertical relation between text and referent with the notion of the book-to-be-continued.

> Realist plotting typically juxtaposes background tableau and foreground *coup de theatre;* realist style typically consists of multiple silhouettings. Realism is a semiosis by silhouetting.

The tracing and retracing of quasi-linguistic mark-
ings on surfaces establish personal identity, but only
from outside, *ex post facto*, and through a draining
tension between the code and its material support.
The repetitious, fixating process of ocular confronta-
tion by which characters recognize themselves and one
another is like the process by which readers recognize
thematic conventions.

And even in Hillis Miller's presidential address I find
the following passage:

The triumph of theory is the resistance to reading
in the sense that theory erases the particularity of the
unique act of reading, but reading itself is always
theoretical in the sense of performing the erasure
and forgetting before we know what is happening
and without our being able to know. So even the
most vigilant and theoretically enlightened reading is
the resistance to reading. Nevertheless, a rhetorically
sophisticated reading is our best hope at least of
remembering that we have forgotten and that we must
forget. For this reason I affirm that the future of literary studies depends on maintaining and developing
that rhetorical reading which today is most commonly
called "deconstruction" [p. 289].

As is true of Miller's address, I am sure that all of the
papers from which I have quoted resulted from intensive study
and profound deliberation. One cannot help but suspect,
however, that lurking behind such passages, which exemplify
the most recent trends in critical theory, is a compulsion not
just to do something spectacular with literature but to write
about it in a language that makes it more serious and thus
somehow more important. "English teachers," notes one English professor, "have proudly erected a segregationist view
that writing of or about literature is unlike all other writing. . . . The greatest need of teachers in our field today is to

end their intolerance of laymen who are ready to believe that professors of literature could have something to say worth saying to others" (Trillin, 1977, p. 88). Another English professor complains that "our critical and scholarly jargons grow more recondite by the day," that "there is something inherently pathetic in a profession that cannot explain its work to the public at least as well as the more articulate scientists manage to explain theirs" (Booth, 1983, p. 321). And yet another observes that "the fear that buzzes most closely around every literary theorist is that he or she is a sort of self-deluding druid, absurdly deploying sequences of magic words that are both unilluminating and ineffectual" (Cheney, 1988, p. 7).

Whatever critical theory is currently in fashion, the stock in trade of English professors, including literary theorists, will always be reading and writing, but I increasingly fear that it will not be about anything if one can no longer read the writing. I continue to see evidence that for English departments the literacy crisis begins at home, that there is a tremendous gap, a grand chasm, between much of what is being written and what, in composition classes, I trust is still being taught about clarity of expression, about the importance of conveying meaning. Had English professors agreed on a goal of self-destruction, then I could understand and applaud such behavior. But I do not think they have agreed on anything of the kind. What immortal hand or eye dared frame this fearful lack of symmetry?

✥ 5 ✣

OTHER LANGUAGES

Communicating
Across Cultures

> *Katherine:* O bon Dieu! les langues des hommes sont
> pleines de tromperies.
>
> *Henry:* What says she, fair one? that the tongues of
> men are full of deceits?
>
> *Alice:* Oui, dat de tongues of de mans is be full of
> deceits.
>
> —William Shakespeare

That in seriously pursuing higher education in an American college or university it is essential to be able to read and write effectively in the English language is not debatable. I at least am not willing to debate it. It does not follow, however, that one need comparable ability in a language other than English. As a result, American universities have long had, and continue to have, a love-hate relationship with the teaching of foreign languages.

Over time many arguments for so doing have been proposed. I am old enough to have attended a high school where the study of Latin was still considered to be an important component of a proper education, partly because it was deemed to be a good intellectual exercise with vaguely defined benefits for learning English grammar, partly because it was within the great tradition of the British public schools. Although there has been an interesting if modest resurgence of Latin in American secondary schools, with persuasive evidence to support the idea that its study does improve skills in reading and writing English, during the past half-century most of the emphasis in the schools and certainly in colleges and universities has been placed on studying a living language, the "commonly taughts" being French, German, Italian, Russian, and Spanish. Spanish college enrollments currently lead French by a considerable margin, French leads German to an even greater extent, and Italian is far behind, barely ahead of Russian. Back in the pack are Latin and Ancient Greek, the former threatening to be passed by Japanese and the latter by Chinese (Brod, 1988, p. 41).

The arguments for studying a second language, whether in secondary or postsecondary schools, have in the latter half of this century shifted from the idea that doing so is the mark of an educated person to more pragmatic arguments, ranging from the hope that lifting the "language curtain" might further international understanding to the plea that language learning is essential for our national security, economic as well as military (Parker, 1966, pp. 110–166). I do not intend to linger over the pragmatic arguments for requiring language study in our schools and colleges, for I am not, in fact, comfortable with many of them.

The idea, for instance, that teaching foreign languages to Americans will help promote international understanding (and thus world peace) is not persuasive. It makes sense only if we are in fact talking about a common language—one that all people speak and understand. Were the world conveniently divided into two or even three or four different languages, then a bi-, tri-, or quadrilingual world would not be outside the realm of possibility. But that is not the case, and even if you take a highly specialized group—say, the 28,000 members of the Modern Language Association—not even one foreign language is shared in common. Chinese, for instance, is a perfectly respectable language, not at all inscrutable to more than a billion people living in the world today, and yet when I served as editor of *PMLA* it would have been ludicrous for me to print an article written in Chinese (or Japanese or

Arabic or Hindi)—ludicrous because the article would have been Greek to all but a handful of the 28,000 MLA members who received it. Indeed, Greek would have been Greek, and even an article written in French or German or Spanish would have been unreadable to as many as half of the MLA members.

If a modern language association in America has to turn to English to assure communication in its publications, why should we think that teaching a myriad of different languages to the American citizenry would encourage world peace through understanding? Even if we all agreed that, say, Italian were to be our first national second language and we expended vast resources to see that all Americans became bilingually Italian, we might (but probably would not) have peace and understanding when in Rome, but what would that do for all the other nations of the world? No, the idea of teaching a foreign language to the "Ugly American" and thereby promoting international goodwill is simply not an impressive argument. Ugly Americans can be just as ugly—in my experience, even more so—when they *do* know the foreign language, especially when they know it badly. Even if one plans to spend ten days each January in say, Acapulco, I do not think that is a good reason for learning Spanish (in Acapulco in January it is sometimes difficult for the American tourist to find someone who speaks Spanish). It is a case of overkill. The reward does not justify the investment, and Berlitz, I suspect, feeds more on good intentions than on language acquisition.

An argument that demands more serious consideration, and one to which I will be turning again later in this chapter, is that America cannot effectively carry on its international business, be that war or peace, without the foreign-language requirement in schools or colleges. Obviously we do need language specialists at various levels in government and industry. How large a number I do not know. I believe that the need is increasing, but, in spite of all the frightening anecdotes about America's inability to function effectively when dealing with foreign diplomats and business leaders, I have seen no indication that either the State Department or IBM is stampeding to hire those language teachers who in recent years have been unable to find suitable employment in academe. On the contrary, a study undertaken by the Rand Corporation a few years ago revealed that "business and industry attach a low priority to language, cultural and area skills, largely because English is so widely used in international business that those skills are rarely essential. When they are, firms have little difficulty in hiring foreign nationals" (Rosenzweig, 1982, p. 124).

I am personally far more comfortable with arguments that center on the idea of language itself. The premise behind such arguments is that we do not know ourselves, know our thoughts or our feelings, unless and until we can effectively formulate them into language. I believe that this is true. For me, language is the open-sesame to the world of ideas—understanding through an awareness of the past, creating through a vision of the future. But language can be tricky, and even our most heightened moments of insight can slip away and vanish unless we capture them in words. "Let me try to explain." "Let me give you an example." "Let me put it another way." "Maybe I can draw you a picture." We struggle to capture "it" through shifting our perspective on the object or action or thought.

How immeasurable the value, then, how immense the enrichment to understanding, in being able to step outside one's native language, step outside one's beliefs and ideas as captured in the idiom of that language, and view the object or action or thought from the perspective and framework of a different vocabulary and structure. To shape one's reality through the tension that evolves from bilingual perspectives, to see the object through two or more language dimensions, sharpens awareness of language, sharpens thought, sharpens reality.

But there is, I think, much more than this, for a language evolves in and through a particular culture, and as we undergo the transformation from one set of codes and symbols and sounds to another, we inevitably take on some of the total experience of the culture and people through which and through whom that language evolved. We view ourselves, our own language and our own culture, through foreign eyes. The goal is not merely to speak Spanish but to gain an understanding of what it means to "be" Spanish. If the strongest argument for a liberal education is ultimately that it enriches understanding through awareness of a broader context, then surely the acquisition of a second language should be an integral part of such an education. While the study of history and literature can give us a valuable perspective through time, the bilingual experience can give us a comparable and equally valuable perspective through space. It is a broadening, an enrichment. It laughs at provincialism. It is the natural enemy of bigotry and prejudice.

Am I saying that a multilingual America would lead to world peace through understanding? No, of course not, but I think that were educated Americans proficient in at least one language in addition to English, we would in fact have taken a significant step toward international understanding through viewing the world and its problems from an enlightened perspective. Moreover, for most students this rationale for language acquisition would probably be more meaningful than any of the pragmatic arguments having to do with employment prospects at some unknown point in their future careers, whether such careers would be concerned with national security or with corporate business interests. This argument also goes far beyond the playing of classroom games with lederhosen, bullfight posters, and Kool-Aid in Gallo wine bottles (Edith Piaf records in background), teasing students with the prospect that they might one day be able to order apéritifs in a Paris café without embarrassment. For in addition to enabling students to gain a deeper awareness of those who speak in other voices and other rooms, acquiring a foreign language would enable them to gain a deeper understanding of themselves.

In any case—and although I live and write this in a city in which probably more different languages are spoken than in any other city in the world—I see no reason to believe that we are about to become multilingual through the teaching of languages to English-speaking Americans in our schools and colleges. While one can (and I soon will) point to some encouraging changes that have recently occurred in language pedagogy, we still have a long way to go merely to recover from the disaster years of the sixties and seventies, to which I must now briefly return.

Although as a high school and college student I on more than one occasion entered into dubious battle with a foreign language, my professional concern with the teaching of languages dates back to 1969, when as chair of UCLA's English department I became involved in a struggle to save the undergraduate foreign-language requirement, which at that time was under siege on my campus and a good many others. Because English was by far the largest of the humanities departments, I felt it my responsibility to organize a "save our F.L.'s" campaign and, having only recently been appointed chair and knowing none of my counterparts in the language departments, I called a solidarity meeting in my office. In that meeting—my indoctrination in working with language professors—I learned firsthand about one of the major difficulties in addressing the foreign-language problem: as new chair of an English department, not only did I not know the chairs of the foreign language departments but they did not know each other.

We tried anyway, and by using all kinds of embarrassing theatrics at meetings of our Academic Senate were able to fend off the enemy for two years. In the end we lost and the requirement was abolished. Our most vocal friends, to my surprise then but not later, were the scientists. What ultimately did us in was opposition from within the language departments themselves. Like those professors of British and American literature who would just as soon see English departments relieved of the responsibility for teaching English composition, a fairly large number of foreign-language professors were interested only in teaching literature and were indifferent to language teaching in general and a language requirement in particular. Let Jorge do it.

Although then and still dominated by professors whose concern is far more with literature than language, the Modern Language Association encompasses all of the modern languages and their literatures, which in theory means everything except Latin and Ancient Greek. When in 1971 I became MLA executive director, I was therefore expected to address the needs of all MLA constituents. Thus a few weeks after taking office I found myself in Washington, appearing before the National Council on the Humanities to speak on "The Plight and Future of Foreign Language Learning in America." What I had to say about the future was singularly uninteresting, but the plight was real enough. This is how I described it to the NEH Council in 1971:

> There are a good many language teachers who, if given the opportunity to say so publicly, would claim that modern foreign languages are on the brink of disaster and are about to descend into the bottomless pit, at the bottom of which are presumably Latin and Greek. Certainly to someone such as the Chairman of a prominent Department of Romance Languages, who in just one year has seen his Spanish and French enrollments drop by 45 percent, the feeling is understandable. Some of the most distinguished and prestigious of our graduate schools have either eliminated or sadly watered down foreign language requirements in the M.A. and even in the Ph.D. program. Foreign language requirements have been abolished, reduced, or modified between 1966 and 1970 in over 45 percent of the B.A.-granting institutions. Between 1968 and 1970, when national enrollments rose 13 percent, enrollments in French and German declined by 7 percent, and there is no reason to suspect that the decline will not continue for the next few years. The situation appears, at least, to be very bleak [1972, p. 5].

Following that presentation and throughout the seventies, the situation actually bleakened, as it had in the case of

English composition. College and university registrations in French, for instance, declined from 388,000 in 1968 to fewer than 250,000 by 1980, in German from 216,000 to 127,000 over the same period, and whereas in 1968 registrations in the modern foreign languages had represented 16.1 percent of total college enrollments, by 1980 that figure had dropped to 7.3 percent (Brod, 1988, p. 43). Some of my more painful and frustrating moments as MLA executive director were therefore spent attempting to unite the many and varied language constituencies in facing a common foe—monolingualism. In so doing, I incessantly rocked my favorite hobbyhorse: a plea to take *acquisition* of a foreign language seriously rather than continuing to impose on students the kind of meaningless course requirement I had defended at UCLA just a few years earlier (Schaefer, 1973b).

Although many American colleges and universities have in recent years been trying to improve their students' communication skills in the English language, few institutions have placed a high priority on assuring that students develop comparable skills in foreign languages. Twenty years ago nearly 90 percent of all colleges and universities required language study, whereas today only 25 percent have a foreign-language requirement for admission and fewer than 60 percent require that their students have knowledge of a foreign language before graduation—and most of those that have retained a language requirement demand merely completion of an elementary sequence of courses or a combination of elementary courses in several languages. In this case a little learning is not a dangerous thing but for most students it is a tedious thing. Because such courses seldom enable a student to use the language with any degree of confidence and thus to enjoy so doing, elementary language courses are seen as little more than obstacle courses on the way to a degree. We must, I have argued and continue to argue, either take language acquisition seriously and require a level of proficiency that will enable a student to use the language, or we should forget the requirement altogether.

The key word is *proficiency,* for without worrying

about its precise definition I am convinced that proficiency and not a set number of courses or of course credits should be the basis for any college or university language requirement. I am of course not alone in so thinking. In the 1980s the "proficiency movement" has dominated discussion in most foreign-language departments. I think it is now being recognized that, more often than not, the traditional course requirement has been a copout, enabling a school to give the impression that studying a language is important without having to ensure that the students actually learn the language. It could, in fact, be argued that the traditional foreign-language requirement is more than any other single factor responsible for the dismal state of languages in our colleges and universities today. "Take two and you're through," as if it were some kind of vaccination. I like to make a comparison to ski schools, where the proficiency concept is used by order of God and nature. Ski schools evaluate individual proficiency before each class by asking you to ski, and either you do it or you do not. You do not move from a Class 3 to a Class 4 skier because you have had a certain number of courses or have passed a certain number of hours in class, whatever the grade received for so doing. You do it because you have mastered skiing at a higher level of proficiency, and to use any other criterion would be, to say the least, unhealthy. We must insist on the student's *learning* a second language, not playing in it.

What inevitably happens with a course requirement is that the course becomes the end in itself, the students being subjected to what is little more than a *der-die-das* dip at the fountain. I passed my high school requirement in Latin (two years), my college undergraduate requirement in Spanish (fifteen hours), and my Ph.D. requirements in French (translating, badly, from an unprepared text) and German (translating from a prepared text, a task at which I succeeded after two attempts only because my examiner was even more inept in English than I was in German). And although on paper I am *muy* multilingual—four foreign languages—the transcript is fraudulent. It was all a game: no meaningful level of proficiency was ever stipulated, or anticipated, or attained. Along with thousands of others, I *der-die-das'*d myself from high school diploma to Ph.D., passed all the requirements, and failed to attain proficiency in any one of the languages I studied.

That is not the way to go. We need, *sorely* need, to develop for our students an acceptable rationale for learning a foreign language. Without that, we are operating in a vacuum. We then need to stipulate a specific level of attainment—one appropriate to the particular major or degree and the particular institution. Ideally, formal instruction should culminate in a "subject matter" class taught in the chosen language, and it would be even more ideal could every student spend a year, or at least a summer, studying abroad. For most institutions this would, however, be unrealistic, and thus attaining proficiency might simply mean that students could, in the language of their choice, read an article in a newspaper no more demanding than, say, the *New York Post,* and then be able to discuss that article with a native speaker. But however ambitious or modest the goal, it must be clearly stated and must be met, without compromise and without exception; it must ensure that the student can gain self-satisfaction by actually *using* the language in some capacity. That is not much to ask, but in the final analysis it is everything.

Since the disaster years of the sixties and seventies, many language departments in schools and colleges have been working to improve their teaching methods, the "direct method" (no English spoken here) having come into vogue in many institutions along with "total immersion" programs at home or abroad. And college enrollments have, however modestly, begun to increase, with registrations in modern foreign languages as a percentage of total college enrollments rising from 7.3 percent in 1980 to 7.8 percent in 1986 (Brod, 1988, p. 41). In the past ten years, however, the most important developments on the foreign-language front have probably occurred outside of academia, beginning in 1978 with President Carter's appointment of the "President's Commission on Foreign Language and International Studies."

This commission's 1979 report, *Strength Through Wisdom*, recognized that "Americans' incompetence in foreign languages is nothing short of scandalous" and that "nothing less is at issue than the nation's security" (pp. 5–6). While most of its far-reaching and costly recommendations were not implemented, the report did dramatically call attention to the problem and thus led to a number of subsequent developments. In 1980, for instance, in its *Humanities in American Life*, the Rockefeller Foundation's Commission on the Humanities strongly urged that language and international studies in schools and colleges be strengthened. In 1983 the National Commission on Excellence in Education's highly publicized and influential *A Nation at Risk* not only supported increased efforts in teaching foreign languages and international studies but went so far as to recommend that the study of foreign languages begin in the elementary grades—a suggestion not seriously proposed since the fifties, when elementary school programs (FLES) were being viewed as a panacea. In 1986 the National Foreign Language Center at the Johns Hopkins University School of Advanced International Studies was created. And, potentially of great significance, efforts are currently under way to introduce legislation in Congress that would authorize a federally funded National Foundation for Foreign Languages and International Studies.

Although, as I have noted above, I have reservations about the validity of the driving force behind this interest, anyone concerned with the state of language learning in America would presumably be encouraged by such developments. There is, however, a serious problem just below the surface, for while the cowman and the farmer may now be friends, the international studies and the foreign-language professions have long been, and continue to be, at odds. Their differences should not—but well may—be irreconcilable.

When, shortly after joining the MLA as executive director, I was asked to speak to the National Council on the Humanities about the plight and future of foreign languages, I shared the platform (it was really a conference table) with Richard Lambert, a sociologist who for the past two decades has been one of the most articulate and active proponents of support for international studies. I was the farmer and—or so it seemed from the perspective of the Modern Language Association—he the cowman, infringing on my turf if not actually usurping my lands. Most language teachers and their various language associations have, in fact, long been suspicious of Lambert and of all those whose interest in languages is from the perspective of international studies (see, for example, Valdés, 1988). And possibly with good reason, for although Lambert has gone to considerable lengths to placate foreign-language teachers, in recognizing "the abysmally low level of foreign language competency of most Americans" he has both antagonized and implicitly blamed the foreign-language profession for the present state of affairs. He has claimed—and from his perspective with some justification—that the skills imparted in our language courses are too low and too "scholastic," that the languages being emphasized are more appropriate for the nineteenth than the twenty-first century, that the means for measuring skill acquisition are outmoded, that the various levels of instruction are not articulated, and that "no one knows or seems concerned about how much of early foreign language training survives to be available for adult use" (Lambert, 1986, pp. 9-10).

The key words here—the red flag for language teachers—are "adult use," for it is clear that Lambert's concern is with our failure to have an adequate number of business leaders, scientists, diplomats, State Department employees, Defense Department officials, and so on with the kind of sophisticated language skills that are desirable when working in the international arena. Such a concern is not unreasonable if one assumes, as did President Carter's commission a decade ago, that America's crisis in foreign languages is primarily a "crisis in national security." Since the launching of Sputnik most of the federal funding in support of language training has in fact come through national defense initiatives in the various NDEA programs, and both the Department of Defense and the Defense Language Institute have been involved in drafting proposals for a National Foundation.

The battle lines are therefore clearly drawn. On one side are the pragmatists, arguing that our highest priority must be to see that those directly involved in international concerns—commercial as well as diplomatic, political, and military—have a high level of proficiency in those languages that at any given time are deemed essential for the nation's prosperity and security. This means concentrating on precisely those languages that in schools, colleges, and universities have long been the "less commonly taughts"—Chinese and Japanese, as well as certain East European, Middle Eastern, and African languages. On the other side are the "commonly taught" language teachers, whose approach to language acquisition is and always has been humanistic, with a strong literary bias. For the truth is that college and university departments in which foreign languages are taught and in which language teachers are trained are at heart literature departments dominated by those whose primary interests are in great books, not great walls.

The battle is, of course, unnecessary. Language teachers need the internationalists as much as the internationalists need them. As I argued in a paper I gave in 1977 at a Georgetown University conference on "Language in American Life," we will never reach the promised land until we recognize that "both the humanistic and the pragmatic arguments for, and approaches to, language learning are valid." It was, and still is, my belief that "the enemy is provincialism, isolationism, monolingualism, and there is no single front on which that enemy can be attacked." But "if we keep the end in mind and recognize that there are many different means to that end, we can all become humanistic pragmatists (or pragmatic humanists) in working together to attain the common goal" (1978, p. 14).

This is very pretty, but it is not, I fear, practical, and thus in recent years I have come to believe that, if the internationalists and the foreign-language teachers are ever to find a common meeting ground, a new approach is necessary. What I have of late been proposing is that, at least in some of our larger universities, the supervision of all language teaching, the "commonlies" as well as the "less commonlies," be delegated to those applied linguists whose concern is pedagogical and whose research is in the teaching of languages per se. Most language departments are horrified at this suggestion, not because of their love for teaching language courses but because they fear that linguists would approach the language as a mechanical exercise devoid of any feeling for or understanding of the culture and literature of the people who speak that language. They also—were one to be perfectly honest—fear that with diminished enrollments their departments would lose faculty positions as well as the teaching assistantships that provide essential support for those of their graduate students who are studying the literature.

I do not share these fears. In my experience, those scholars whose careers are devoted to pedagogy, to finding more effective methods for teaching languages, are quite as likely to have a deep feeling for and understanding of the culture behind a given language as are professors in language departments whose interests are in an author or a period centuries removed from the current scene. Moreover, I am merely advocating that the teaching of the elementary and intermediate courses be *supervised* by applied linguists. Courses could continue to be taught, as in most large institutions they are at present, by untenured lecturers or by graduate students enrolled in the various language departments. In some language departments, perhaps in many, the teaching of the language is given high priority and is done superbly, but in others it simply is not given high priority and is far less effective than it might be. Indeed, in many of our large universities the individual who supervises language instruction, as is true of those who oversee composition courses in an English department, is a second-class citizen to whom recognition (including tenure) is awarded, if awarded at all, grudgingly. I am increasingly convinced that delegating supervision of language instruction to those applied linguists whose research is in language pedagogy would, in many institutions, dramatically improve the instruction and, not incidentally, meet the needs of internationalists for greater emphasis on teaching the "less commonlies" while still preserving traditional interests in the "commonlies."

I continue to believe, however, that until colleges and universities insist that their students develop a reasonable level of proficiency in at least one foreign language and then create within their institutions the means whereby students can effectively employ their acquired skills, no approach to instruction, wherever centered and however undertaken, will be much more effective than what we have at present.

I am not naive as regards the inherent difficulties in taking language acquisition seriously. Acquiring a new language, while relatively easy for a child, is difficult for the vast majority of adults. As we learned time and again through military and Peace Corps programs, the key to language acquisition is motivation, and, in light of the dominance of English in our country, that is hard to come by. On the European continent college and high school students do not learn a second (or third or fourth) language because they are brighter than American students but because they perceive that they will have occasion to use the language. Were we to insist that all college graduates attain even an intermediate level of proficiency in just one foreign language and were we to ensure that the language would actually be *used* by students, not just in their language classes or in extracurricular programs but in their humanities or social science courses, we would have gone a long way in providing that motivation. It may not be quite as simple as all that, but it is also not as difficult as we have long made it out to be. The rewards in so doing, for society and for the individual, would, I believe, be immense.

❧ 6 ❧

TEACHING
AND LEARNING

Awakening
the Need to Know

A teacher affects eternity; he can never tell where his
influence stops.

What one knows is, in youth, of little moment; they
know enough who know how to learn.

—Henry Adams

I began this book by suggesting that the educational process
can be reduced to a simple X-Y-Z formula. A teacher knows
something (or knows how to do something) that a student
wants to know (or know how to do), and thus X teaches Y
to Z. For the educational process to succeed, however, teachers
must be willing to share their skills or knowledge with the
students and, I would add, enjoy so doing. Equally important
is that the students genuinely desire to learn whatever it is
that their teachers are prepared to teach. Chaucer added the
key ingredient in noting that his clerk would gladly learn
and gladly teach.

A good deal of time and effort has been spent in worrying about today's generation of students, trying to ascertain
how, if at all, they differ from earlier generations and attempting to determine whether whatever differences are perceived

have made them better or worse. Obviously there have been
changes. There are, for instance, far more college students
today than there were forty years ago—many millions more—
and they are more diverse in terms of age, race, and ethnic
origin. As I have suggested in earlier chapters, in terms of
acquired knowledge as well as skills they are also notably less
prepared to undertake a college education. But having spent
most of my adult life—some forty years—in or around institutions of higher education, I have concluded that the fundamental differences between young students of the forties,
sixties, and eighties are not that great.

We have, to be sure, witnessed superficial changes in
dress, in vocabulary, in eating habits, maybe in what appears
to be (but I suspect in reality is not) sophistication in things
sexual. Yet the kids who in the forties rented white tuxedos to
attend proms with the big bands share in common with the
Woodstock crowds, beads and all, as well as the more recent
antiapartheid constructors of shanties, the simple fact that
they were doing their thing, that they were "relating," that
they were discovering themselves in the social milieu within
which they found themselves. In evaluating a particular generation of undergraduate students as being active or passive,
altruistic or solipsistic, dedicated or indifferent, we fail to
recognize that most of these kids—and I exclude the increasingly large number of older students returning to college—
are at a stage in their lives when they are more interested in
being and belonging than in becoming.

Of far greater importance, I have also failed to notice
much difference in young students as regards their attitude
toward learning—the acquisition of genuine intellectual curiosity—which is the one thing needful in pursuing an education at any level. Over the years I have perhaps detected some
minor differences among college and university campuses in
what one might call the "intellectual milieu." As a student at
the University of Chicago during the Hutchins years, I recall
thinking that even the graffiti in the men's room was intel-
lectually stimulating; and when I taught a seminar at Columbia in 1974 I found the students to be intensely serious—

obnoxiously so—although that impression was enhanced when I recently discovered that the best graduate student in my 1974 seminar is, some fifteen years later, still a Columbia graduate student. But as regards the desire on the part of most young students to gladly learn, I cannot say that I have detected significant change.

On the contrary, the survey of UCLA undergraduate students I referred to in Chapter Two revealed that students have no more and possibly less intellectual curiosity than had my freshman classmates at the University of Missouri more than forty years ago. Although today's UCLA students are, by most measures, as good as they come, the survey revealed that fewer than half (43 percent) claimed to talk frequently with a faculty member, that only a quarter frequently visited with their instructors after class, that only about 20 percent frequently made an appointment to meet with faculty in their offices or to discuss with them their ideas for a term paper. Equally depressing, the survey revealed that some 42 percent of the students never talked to other students about art, 40 percent never talked with each other about theater, only 37 percent talked frequently with other students about social problems, and only 27 percent talked frequently with other students about scientific theories and methods. And although UCLA has a large number of foreign students, 37 percent of the undergraduates admitted that they had never had a serious discussion with students from other countries. If, as Alexander Astin claims, student involvement is the key to effective education, on at least these scores education at UCLA would appear to leave a good deal to be desired (1985, pp. 133–157).

Depending on the campus, there are obviously vast differences in opportunities for students to interact with other students and with faculty members. Compare, for instance, a large urban commuter university such as UCLA with a small liberal arts college such as Kenyon or Antioch. Nevertheless, I have no reason to believe that the situation on my campus is much different from most of today's colleges and universities, where, as they did in the forties and the sixties, students still tend to answer the question, "What did you get out of that course?" with a letter of the alphabet. I suspect that the fragmented nature of most undergraduate programs is a major factor in discouraging the exchange of ideas, there being no necessity for friends to be taking the same or even similar courses concurrently, which is one of the many reasons I advocate a single general education program during a student's first two years in college. But I think there is another, even more important reason for this lack of intellectual curiosity— the failure in both schools and colleges to teach students how to study, how to think, how to learn, how, in short, to become actively involved in their education. Desire is not enough. Other things are also essential to the educational process, and for most students they do not come naturally.

Because we have not done a very good job in teaching students how to write, this failure in teaching them how to think and study is perhaps not surprising. There is, I contend, a close relationship between the ability to write and the ability to think. But the fact remains that, at least in my experience, few undergraduates have learned how to explore ideas, how to walk around an issue, to debate it, to see what makes it tick—and to enjoy so doing. I recall during my year at the University of London how students would delight in debating an issue—*any* issue—and be willing to argue heatedly on either or both sides of the question. In contrast, when teaching Joyce's *Portrait of the Artist* in one of my courses last year, I found that the students were incredulous (in fact, they laughed) when I suggested that the debates about esthetics that Stephen Dedalus and his friends engaged in were no doubt much like those they hold each night in their dormitories. And I shall never forget the horrified look on the faces of my freshman students when, during one of the presidential elections a few years ago, I asked them to write at the top of their papers the name of the candidate they supported and then develop a polemical essay persuading me to vote for the other candidate. A bumper-sticker mentality cannot handle that kind of assignment. And we still have, I fear, a vast number of bumper-sticker students.

All students, I hasten to add, are not like that. There are today thousands of extraordinary young people attending American colleges who have learned how to learn, learned how to work within the system, and thus are truly profiting from their educational experience. Over the years I have been fortunate in meeting with many of them, especially during my years in administration, when most of those I encountered were honor students, candidates for Rhodes scholarships, class presidents, and such. Indeed, in 1984–85 some of these UCLA students, deeply concerned about the quality of their own education, organized a two-day conference to discuss the recently published national reports critical of undergraduate education and then wrote a provocative fifty-two-page report of their own, aptly titled *A Need for Reform.* Unfortunately, such students are the exceptions. The vast majority of the 12.3 million students currently enrolled in American colleges and universities neither take nor know how to take full advantage of their educational opportunities.

The survey mentioned above revealed that 60 percent of UCLA's students, all of whom are theoretically attending school on a full-time basis, spend thirty hours a week or less in their classes and studying, and 70 percent of those students claim to receive grades of B or better. Perhaps the students participating in that survey were being modest, underestimating the effort they put into their education. My fear, however, is that the opposite is true, not just at UCLA but at most colleges and universities, and this is only in part because, as I suggested in my first chapter, the sideshows tend to dominate the activities in the main ring. There are, of course, exceptions. One thinks of liberal arts colleges such as Reed or Williams and private universities such as Dartmouth or Chicago. But for the most part, on American college and university campuses we have not attained or maintained the kind of intellectual milieu that is essential if the educational process is to flourish. Unless and until we do, the answer to the question, "How high is higher education?" will continue to be, "Not very."

Undergraduate students frequently argue that the problem is with poor teaching, and they are surely not alone in so doing, as we were constantly reminded by William Bennett during his tenure as secretary of education and in numerous reports emanating from national committees and commissions. The following comment from *Integrity in the College Curriculum* is typical: "Research, not teaching, pays off in enhanced reputation, respect of peers beyond one's own campus, and access to funds. The language of the academy is revealing: professors speak of teaching *loads* and research *opportunities*, never the reverse" (Association of American Colleges, 1985, p. 10). And that, I fear, is true. But while concern with the quality of teaching and the importance, or lack of importance, placed on it in colleges and universities continues, the sad fact of the matter is that with few exceptions no serious effort has been or is being made to teach college and university teachers how to teach.

In a paper I delivered in 1977 to a group of English department chairs ("Still Crazy After All These Years"), I argued that during the critical decade of the sixties English departments had a flawless record in that they had managed to do everything wrong and nothing right. Among the deadliest of the seven sins they had committed was to ignore teaching and teacher training. What I said then, and still believe to be true, is this:

> Of all our sins, the most difficult to understand, to explain to ourselves or to the public, was our reluctance in the 1960s to ensure that the teachers we were producing in unprecedented numbers could actually teach. Perhaps it had something to do with our faith in the written word, the naive belief that having said it in print would suffice. Perhaps it was the image of the professor as one who professes, a kind of knowledge machine into which students could drop their pennies to receive answers, rather than the image of one who goes forth to spread good tidings and attract disciples. Perhaps it was simply that, having paid so

> little attention to their own teaching, it just never
> occurred to departments that they might create a new
> generation that would teach. Whatever the reason,
> those thousands upon thousands of new Ph.D. recip-
> ients in the 1960s met their first classes with only the
> fuzziest notion of what they were doing there. As it
> always has, the law of averages dictated that some of
> these young people would have the talent and the
> instinct to develop into effective teachers, and they
> did and they have. Perhaps the best we can say about
> the rest is that they were sincere [p. 3].

In the late sixties and early seventies, as a panacea for
all the ills that at that time beset college and university teaching, there was a brief but serious revival of interest in graduate
programs leading to the doctor of arts degree. Such programs,
while including most of the traditional coursework for a
Ph.D. degree, added what were sometimes called "tool" or
"how to" courses, and they usually replaced the dissertation
with a teaching internship prior to awarding the degree.
Although much of the interest was in training teachers for
the rapidly growing number of community and junior colleges, there was also reason to believe that excessive specialization of the Ph.D. had led to less than scintillating classroom
performances in four-year colleges and universities. Among
advocates of the D.A. degree there was growing suspicion that
the problems of the sixties had been caused not so much by
teaching having been irrelevant as by its having been inept.

While the D.A. degree seemed to some to promise
a reasonable and fairly quick fix, the debate that ensued
between proponents of the Ph.D. and those of the D.A.
was heated and short-lived, and its outcome was predictable
(Schaefer, 1973a). Universities do many things well, but, as
I have already suggested, they excel when it comes to resist-
ing change. The best-laid plans for most of the "teaching"
degrees never really had a chance.

I am not sure that such degrees would have made much
difference. Training good scholars is difficult enough, and

with all the emphasis we have placed on scholarship in doctoral programs we are still not very successful at it. But developing good teachers is even more difficult. There are some obvious things graduate departments can do to assist their students in becoming more effective teachers, and some are doing them. Some graduate programs, for instance, now try to give all of their Ph.D. candidates an opportunity to prepare classes, to deliver lectures, or to lead discussion sections in large lecture courses under the supervision of an experienced professor. Some arrange informal meetings at which graduate students and the department's most effective teachers share ideas on what works and does not work in the classroom. A few departments have made arrangements for apprentice programs with local two-year colleges, enabling graduate students to get additional teaching experience before completing their degrees.

Such efforts are surely to be applauded and encouraged, but they are limited in that they do not, and almost certainly could not, alter the personality—the style, if you will—of the individual teacher. Some people, teachers included, *are* dull, and nothing, at least nothing that could reasonably be undertaken in a graduate degree program, will alter that situation. Dull teachers are not, however, necessarily bad teachers. In teaching, one need not sparkle to be brilliant, although most of today's undergraduates, having been weaned on the tube, seem to expect that a really good teacher will look and sound like Judy Woodruff or Dan Rather. I have come to believe, however, that what is frequently condemned as bad teaching is often due simply to the institution's having arranged or permitted unhappy marriages between teacher, student, subject, the kind or size of class, or all of these combined. The sad thing is that while the unhappiest of these relationships could easily be avoided, few colleges or universities do so or, I suspect, even recognize that the possibility to do so exists.

It is not true that there are no bad teachers or poor students. There are. But I have concluded that much of what is called bad teaching results from assigning a perfectly respectable teacher to the wrong course. Asking faculty members to teach courses in which they know little more than their best students is stupid. Whatever else it may involve, good teaching requires knowledge. That is a given, a prerequisite; and when faculty, whether in schools or colleges, are assigned to courses that they are less than qualified to teach, the end result will be bad teaching. That such assignments not infrequently occur through necessity ("Our Shakespeare specialist is on leave. What am I to do?") does not alter the fact that the student is cheated. Better to not offer the course than to offer it with someone marginally qualified to teach it.

Equally disastrous is to ask even a highly qualified teacher to handle a class for which, in terms of number of students or level of instruction, that person is temperamentally unsuited. Research universities are especially vulnerable here; they often find that they have hired brilliant introverts who are superb at conducting graduate seminars and directing doctoral dissertations but are pathetic when attempting (microphone dangling from the neck) to teach an introductory course to a class of hundreds. Two of the finest seminars I had as a graduate student were taught by superb teachers who were, to say the least, ill at ease in an undergraduate lecture course. Perfect scheduling can probably never be achieved, but putting the right players in the right position can make a tremendous difference.

Viewing the problem from the student's perspective and assuming that most really do want to take courses that interest them, I have come to believe that course descriptions in college catalogs are of little assistance. If one can judge from all the "drops" and "adds" that occur on today's campuses, in selecting courses students apparently miss as often as they hit. While there is no substitute for a strong advising program, detailed descriptions of each course and its instructor could be (but usually are not) made available through the departments, and students could be (but seldom are) encouraged to visit classes they think they might want to take prior to the term in which they plan to enroll. Of equal importance is that students select instructors whose approach to teaching is compatible with their own approach to learning. There are excellent students who prefer to have class time devoted exclusively to words of wisdom from their professor. The last thing they want is classroom discussion in which time is spent listening to obvious answers to what seem to them to be dumb questions. There are also, however, students for whom happiness is being able to talk in class and who seem to profit most from a course when they are able to participate. The trick is to match these various desires, and that can be done through careful advising, descriptions written by instructors explaining how they conduct their classes, or class visits prior to enrollment.

These things can help, can in many instances make a considerable difference. But we will still have student complaints about bad teachers and bad teaching as long as students fail to recognize that effective teaching does not always or necessarily produce immediate results. Whether students realize it or not, very often the melody lingers on and what at the time seemed to be a less than scintillating educational experience proved in the long run to be rewarding. In a liberal education the learning process frequently transcends both the subject and the teacher.

As a student, I never had a course that I did not like or that I remembered much about a year later. What I learned about frogs from a professor in an introductory zoology course at the University of Missouri has long been forgotten, along with the name of that professor. What in the long run I learned from that course was that even frogs, when presented by someone who knows about both frogs and undergraduate students, can be fascinating. What I memorized in a British history course at NYU I have for the most part forgotten. What I learned is that history is, or can be, inseparable from literature. But immediately upon completing these and any number of other courses I might mention, I would never have identified what I now recognize to be what I "got out of" those courses.

From the teacher's perspective I have also concluded that there is no way of knowing when one has succeeded, when or if the student's achievement has become the teacher's triumph. A few years ago I met a reporter from the *Los Angeles Times* who, upon learning of my association with UCLA, proceeded to tell me in no uncertain terms about all the stupid courses he had taken there. He could, in fact, remember only one truly good course in his four years as an undergraduate. He could not remember the name or even the face of his professor, but as he continued to describe in remarkable detail what went on in that course, including the precise wording of some examination questions that were indelibly impressed on his mind, it became clear that the course was mine, that I had been his teacher. It would seem that, like the gods, teaching and learning work in mysterious ways their wonders to perform. One never really knows when it happened, or if, or how.

But to return to the lack of intellectual curiosity in today's students, if the problem cannot be blamed solely on teachers or teaching, I sometimes suspect that to a great extent it is due to our obsession with grades and to the immense importance placed on grade-point averages (GPAs), whether used for admission to college or graduate school, in competition for fellowships and scholarships, or even in the marketplace. Recognizing this, a few colleges and universities have eliminated grades, which only means that for those students who want to pursue graduate work in other institutions the instructors must assign what are in effect "prose grades," often-lengthy essays that are inevitably translated into a grade-point average by the graduate schools to which such students apply ("This one sounds like a B+ to me"). One recent comprehensive study that attempts to "make sense of college grades" actually recommends (without much hope that its recommendation will be adopted) that the "meaningless" GPA be abolished entirely (Milton, Pollio, and Eison, 1986, pp. 218–223).

But if eliminating grades or grade-point averages is not practical, we would at least be somewhat better off were we to recognize and to persuade all concerned that the grade is not the goal, that in pursuing a liberal education what one gets out of a course is frequently subjective and therefore cannot be effectively measured on a comparative basis. When an outstanding student, one who has consistently written sensitive and perceptive essays on assigned poems, in class and out, stops short in the middle of an examination, scratches out what she has written, and scrawls, "I'm sorry, Dr. Schaefer, but this poem is too important to me to bullshit about it," what do I do? Fail her? Reduce her course grade? No, of course not. It does not work that way. Grades are all well and good in vocational training. Whether a professional is operating on my carburetor or my heart, I want assurance that through extensive testing such an individual has been certified to be able to perform the act successfully. When the student is pursuing a liberal education, I could not care less. But as long as the students care, as long as we compel them to care, learning as process will be lessened.

However that may be, and returning to an earlier theme, I am convinced that the single most important reason for our failure to have created a campus climate in which a love of learning is dominant is that we have allowed our students to think of college primarily in terms of career opportunities, have let them believe that the answer to the question, "Why go to college?" is, as our friends at CUNY answered it, "To get a better job." As a result, students tend to view their college experience not as an end in itself, an extraordinary opportunity to spend four or five or more years freely indulging in intellectual endeavor, but simply as a means to an end, a rite of passage through which one must pass before entering the real world. And such an attitude is not, I fear, a new one. If students of the eighties do not, as I have argued, differ significantly, at least in terms of intellectual curiosity, from those of the sixties and the forties, the failure to differentiate between a liberal education and training for a career may indeed be the overriding reason.

In spite of what I have earlier suggested was an encouraging trend to restore "education" to a college education, this has not yet happened, and I am not sanguine that it will occur in the immediate future. I do, however, see one small ray of hope as the result of a very different kind of change that has begun to occur in the way students are being taught and in the way they learn and study. I see the possibility (it is far from a certainty) that this change could alter not just how we teach or how students learn but the entire fabric of higher education. I speak, of course, of the computer.

From talking wrist watches to space shuttles, from computerized chess to the Bodleian in a boob tube, we have begun to experience what many of us suspect is the most important revolution in human history. The tools even now at our disposal are so overwhelming in their complexity that we can only grope for an understanding of their implications, of what they mean for information retrieval or communication, of how they affect memory, thought, free will, the right to be wrong, to be what we call human. And this is just the beginning. Where it will lead in the coming century, and where it will end, no one knows.

It is not my intention to speculate on what form educational applications of the computer will ultimately take. I am willing to accept the idea that by the end of this century all colleges and universities will be "computer-intensive," whatever that may ultimately mean (and it will, I suspect, mean a very great deal). What interests me more than the technology are the ways in which the computer could ultimately enhance the intellectual milieu of a campus—unlikely as that might seem at first glance—and could conceivably change what today's students have come to expect from a college education.

Computers do many things well, but there are two things they do superbly, far better than we mortals. One is to serve as a data bank, providing us with a kind of collective memory in which can be stored "facts." If what we want is to know what happened, if it is "true," we can now call the spirits from the vasty deep and be assured that they will come when we do call them. The other thing computers do much better than we noncomputers is to teach certain kinds of skills—not because computers are more sensitive as teachers but because they can be programmed to know more, they can function tirelessly day and night, and they possess infinite patience. They are also fun, and thus I have no doubt but that today's third-graders, the Star Wars generation, will find it easier and far more pleasant to learn to spell on a CRT than did my generation under the loving tutelage of she-of-the-squeaky-chalk. It seems possible, then, given a generation of college students programmed to think of higher education in terms of how to do something, that much of the "how to do" could become "how to use the computer to do" or "how to have the computer teach us to do" whatever one's vocationally oriented heart desires.

What might happen were hard-core vocational training to be undertaken largely through computer applications? More than that, what might happen were such training to be undertaken, as it increasingly is, by the employers, by the firms themselves? What I have in mind goes beyond the proprietary schools and into what is often called the third tier of the educational enterprise—TWA providing its own school for training in the TWA way; Citibank teaching all one needs to know to be a Citibank clerk; Holiday Inn training its own managers; Hughes Aircraft, its own engineers; Merrill Lynch, its own stockbrokers. This already exists, a twentieth-century version of the eighteenth-century apprenticeship. If the "how to" expectations could be met—and met more effectively and efficiently—outside of academe, what is it that colleges and universities would have to offer a class of "how to" students? What would be left for colleges and universities beyond the homecoming game and the spring sing?

My hope, of course, is that were such changes to occur, even in small measure, students might come to expect something different from their college experience, to have great expectations moving beyond the "how to" syndrome, moving even beyond the question, "Is it true?" to the far more interesting question, "What does it mean?" After a long period of emphasizing *doing*, higher education could begin a new period of *knowing*, an active passivity that would explore meaning and place the emphasis on connections, on correspondences, on relating facts and skills to self and to self in social interaction with other selves. What I am describing is of course akin to the kind of liberal education I have argued for in previous chapters, but fantastically enriched and enhanced.

Imagine a college experience in which "background," whatever the subject, would primarily be acquired not in lecture halls with hundreds of students sitting in uncomfortable chairs taking inaccurate notes but through interactive computer programs and video discs, and with such background being viewed merely as preparation for a higher kind of education. Then imagine a college experience in which students so prepared would interact not with machines but with small groups of other students and with a sensitive instructor in discovering by and for themselves what things mean. Knowledge exists. It is readily available. To make it real, to make it meaningful, it must be absorbed by a human intelligence, be transformed into what Arnold called a "spontaneity of consciousness." The university could of course continue to be a center for research and a place where graduate training is provided in certain esoteric professions such as law, but above all the university would be the place wherein all knowledge, all disciplines, all professions, all skills are connected and in which one might turn to a new generation of teachers and students for that which we have increasingly forgotten to ask: for wisdom.

Most of the students who will enter college in the first decade of the next century are today in their cribs, some still wandering between two worlds waiting for the miracle to happen. I think it is at least possible that the colleges and universities they will enter will be different from the ones I attended—so different in degree that they could actually be different in kind. I also suspect that if the kind of change I have described is to occur it will happen quietly—almost, at first, without our realizing it. It may, in fact, already be happening.

I see no reason to believe that either students or teachers have changed much in this century or that they promise to do so in the next. What *could* change is how teachers, human or machine, go about teaching whatever it is that students want to know or know how to do. Within our colleges and universities, such a change could make a considerable difference in what we call an education. It is a consummation devoutly to be wished, and I for one wish it.

✌ 7 ☙

PUBLISHING,
PERISHING

They Also Serve
Who Only Teach

'Tis pleasant, sure, to see one's name in print;
A book's a book, although there's nothing in't.
——George Gordon, Lord Byron

I am not sure when it happened, but at some time in the
postwar years (was it in the sixties? surely not much earlier
than that) some of our larger and more prominent universities gradually, if quite unofficially, became "research universities." No one, to my knowledge, planned this. Language
works in mysterious ways and the term was not, after all,
inappropriate, given that the institutions so self-designated
were those in which organized research, especially labora-
tory research in the sciences and health sciences, was a major
part of their mission. By 1973 the Carnegie Council on Policy Studies in Higher Education had, in any case, made the
label official by designating some ninety-two institutions as
"Research Universities." Whatever the origins of the label,
the word *research*, especially with a capital letter, enhanced
the prestige of such universities and the term was therefore
readily adopted.

What is in a name? Probably not all that much, unless
one begins to take it too seriously or, in this case, too literally.

I doubt if anyone in the sciences, the health sciences, or even those areas of the social sciences that are more scientific than social noticed any change when universities that were engaged in organized research became research universities. Where I think it perhaps made a subtle difference was in those areas of the university in which dissemination more than discovery had long been the driving force and, were one to be perfectly honest, the *raison d'être*. However it came about—and the name is surely more symptom than cause— the fact is that today all faculty members in a research university, whether in an academic or a professional department, are expected to "do" research and to publish their discoveries. This is, moreover, increasingly the case even in those four-year colleges and universities whose missions do not now include and never have included organized research. One of the most alarming findings in Ernest Boyer's *College* is that between 1975 and 1984 the percentage of faculty who found that it was difficult to achieve tenure without publishing increased from 54 percent to 69 percent, which no doubt explains why over the same period the percentage whose interests tended toward teaching as opposed to research declined from 70 percent to 63 percent and the percentage who had published a book or monograph increased from 38 percent to 45 percent (1987, pp. 129-130).

In juxtaposing dissemination with discovery, I of course have in mind primarily those humanistic disciplines in which, in olden days, much of what was being done was *dissemination* in the classroom—a word that, as I am using it, is just a fancy name for teaching. Indeed, in the fifties some of the finest professors I studied with had little to show in the way of publications, and I can think of several who had important things to say to their students about history, literature, or philosophy and said them, in what later became known as research universities, without Ph.D. degrees. What they also had was a love of their subject and a commitment to share that love with their students.

I also have no idea, nor do I really care, when the term "publish or perish" came into the language, although

I would guess that prior to the fifties it was not nearly as
prominent as it is today. In using the term, one usually thinks
of young assistant professors who, in the six, seven, or eight
years of their apprenticeship, must do extraordinary things
in print or suffer the indignity of termination. In my experience, however, to perish by not getting tenure in one of
the humanistic disciplines is often not as painful as having
reached the promised land only to realize that one must
continue doing more—in quantity if not necessarily quality—of whatever one did to gain entrance in the first place.
Being fired is a one-time event, and it is possible to alleviate
the pain in a number of ways—by getting another job, for
instance. But for those tenured professors who are dedicated
to teaching and devoted to their students and who are never
advanced beyond the lowest tenure ranks because they have
in good conscience been unwilling or unable to play the
game, "publish or perish" has even more profound meaning:
it is a form of slow death.

As a graduate student in English I was aware that my
professors published articles and occasionally books, and I
knew that were I to become one of them, I would no doubt be
expected to do the same. And I did, publishing several very
scholarly articles, a number of witty and appropriately nasty
book reviews, a ground-breaking monograph on a minor nineteenth-century poet, and an edition of that poet's prose, for
all of which I was granted tenure and eventually a full profes-
sorship. It was not, however, until I became executive director
of the Modern Language Association and, as such, editor of
its premier publication, *PMLA*, that I began to understand
the enormity of the publication game, at least as it is played
in the humanistic disciplines.

In assuming the editorship of *PMLA* I inherited a two-
year backlog of articles that my predecessor had accepted for
publication. The journal at that time had no editorial board
and thus the editor, aided by consultant readers, was to all
intents and purposes both judge and jury. No doubt all of
the articles about to appear in print exemplified impeccable
scholarship, but it struck me that they were perhaps some-

what limited in their appeal, perhaps a bit too specialized for a journal that all 28,000 MLA members, at least those who had paid their dues, received four times a year. No doubt "Perspectives on Harold Frederic's *Market-Place*," "Dancourt's Regency Plays," and "Structure and Symbol in Manzoni's *I Promessi Sposi*" would be read with interest by the handful of members interested in Frederic, Dancourt, or Manzoni. But it occurred to me that it might make more sense, given *PMLA*'s circulation—which was then and still is ten times greater than even the most successful of other scholarly journals in the field—to print only articles of such importance that they would simply have to be read by anyone with pretensions to a serious interest in literary scholarship, regardless of one's field of specialization or research interests.

Shortly after I assumed office, then, the MLA executive council approved my proposal for a new editorial policy in keeping with that concept. With it the council also approved the creation of a seven-member editorial board that would hold meetings four times a year to work with me in selecting articles deemed good enough and important enough, regardless of subject or approach, to justify their being brought to the attention of some 28,000 (potential) readers. In the future, *PMLA* would be printing only articles "of significant interest to the entire membership."

As I have already suggested, such was not the case in prior years, when it was extremely unlikely that anyone except the editorial staff and the committee charged with selecting the best article of the year ever read all of the articles in any single issue. Reactions to the old *PMLA* had, in fact, been less than enthusiastic, the attitudes being accurately reflected in a survey undertaken in 1969 by a special MLA commission, which reported that the advertisements and the "professional notes" in the back of each issue were the only part of *PMLA* to receive any praise at all. One reader called the journal "big, stuffy, and dull," another used the words "pedantic, uninspiring, and a waste of money," another said simply, "*PMLA* is a horrible magazine," and yet another felt that "most of the articles in *PMLA* remind me of an Aubrey

Beardsley sultan, aloof and tragically obese in silly clothes. Who but the sultan can have the charity to care if a soul lies swamped somewhere in that bulbous mass?"

The new editorial policy was announced in March 1973 with mild fanfare and to a few guffaws. We began receiving submissions soon thereafter and in January 1975 printed the first of the new articles. The reaction, which warmed my childish scholarly heart, was as astonishing as it was favorable. From Ohio: "The first new *PMLA* seems to me really very different and very good." From Illinois: "I very much approve of the new policy. I've stopped throwing the issues away." From Connecticut: "No longer is *PMLA* just a certain number of ounces of paper appearing inevitably in one's mailbox! For the first time in my years of MLA membership, I look forward to its arrival." And from New York: "The new *PMLA* has become an exciting magazine, has a spirit of adventure lacking before. Marvellous!"

During the first two years under the new policy we received more than 1,200 submissions, around 1,000 of which met the basic criteria (such as length and format) and were acceptable for processing. This meant that each of those 1,000 articles was sent to a consultant specialist, who wrote a report that was then forwarded, along with the article, to one of eighteen members of an advisory committee. Both readers were asked to determine whether the article was of such significance as to justify further consideration, and if those two readers disagreed a third opinion was sought. With two favorable votes the article then went to the editorial board, which ultimately decided if the article was appropriate under the new policy.

Of the first 1,000 articles on which final action was taken, the answer to that question was a resounding 95 percent no. From the 1,000 articles submitted over a two-year period we found only 53 deemed good enough and important enough to publish under the new editorial policy, and, truth be told, at least half of the fifty-three were really not that good. The dreary fact of the matter is that from 1,000 articles presumably submitted under the impression that the work was important and of significant interest to all literary scholars, we were able to identify perhaps 30 that were truly worth bringing to the attention of the entire profession. After the success of the first few issues, we struggled with the problem for five years, receiving fewer and fewer articles that qualified for publication. Shortly after I left office in 1978, my new editorial policy was abandoned.

At first I could not understand why, in a profession of such size and presumed stature, with the oldest and most prestigious journal in the field promising speedy publication, we were not overwhelmed with outstanding articles. It was, of course, possible that the best work, work that would indeed have been of significant interest to the entire profession, was appearing in other periodicals. Another possibility was that literary scholars had increasingly focused their research on specialized topics of interest only to those who shared their concerns, and thus our best work was simply not appropriate for the new policy. A third possibility was that literary scholars had grown so accustomed to the idea that their work would be read by only a relatively small number of specialists, if read at all, that they simply never thought of communicating their ideas to a broader audience. But it was the fourth possibility that I began to suspect was the most likely—the possibility that the mass production of English and foreign-language Ph.D.'s in the sixties had done more than just produce unprepared teachers and create serious problems of unemployment. It had produced a generation of scholar-teachers who were only half-trained and had only a half-baked notion of what scholarship was all about. As W. Jackson Bate has put it, "The profession engorged a huge group—mostly all tenured now—who regarded literature as a private preserve, and were themselves innocent of history, of philology, of 'ideas' generally" (1982, p. 50).

What follows are excerpts from some of the comments made by those who read articles submitted to *PMLA* under my ill-fated policy. The comments have been selected at random, with the names of the authors omitted.

On D. H. Lawrence: This article has two major de-
fects: the discussion [of a work by another author]
adds nothing to our understanding of Lawrence and
does not serve as a significant exemplar; the description of Lawrence's omniscient technique is faulty and,
in the extended case of *Sons and Lovers,* inaccurate.
The surprising and perverse conclusion might well
have led [the author] to question the essential validity
of the argument to begin with.

On Gothic romance: Although [the author] makes
some interesting points along the way, his essay depends upon inconsistent, arbitrary, and unconvincing
distinctions among genres. Most disturbing of all is
his presenting his argument in a scholarly vacuum.
He seems unaware that anyone else has ever considered the genre.

On Burton's Anatomy of Melancholy: The essay is
uneven in quality. I guess problems always occur
when an author decides to spend a lot of energy
attacking another critic rather than simply attending
to the text.

On Proust: There is a degree of critical naivete involved in asking whether Proust's novel is essentially
a "happy" or a "suffering" text, and seriously arguing for the one over the other. The catalogue of pain
and suffering hardly ever gets beyond the obvious.
The assumed christology in the portrayal of the protagonist is preposterous. The failure to distinguish
between author, narrator, and protagonist is another
methodological weakness.

On Humphrey Clinker: [The author] has not turned
up any results—at least results that I can see—worthy
of publication. Literary scholarship, like other empir-
ical endeavors, sometimes does not yield results, and

when that happens perhaps the proper response is to look elsewhere.

On Pinter and Chekhov: The article's most significant limitation is its failure to reveal, by means of the comparisons drawn, anything fresh and finally significant about the plays themselves. The comparison here made is apt, but it is not worth undertaking (except as a classroom device) unless it illumines the works in some new way.

On Leopardi: The paper's only claim to interest lies in its subject, not in the treatment of that subject. How the paper could be improved? Substitute analysis for summaries of works, rethink completely the relevance and hierarchy of the secondary sources used, and reorganize the presentation to give it some intellectual "punch" instead of this rather drab marshaling of evidence.

On Milton: [The author] should reconsider his intention to publish this piece as an article. There are some possibilities here for a couple of notes, perhaps. As an article, this is repetitious and needlessly inflated. It does not seem suitable for *PMLA* and cannot help either [the author] or any other scholarly journal that would consider publishing it.

These were not comments on papers written in elementary composition courses or by undergraduate English majors or by graduate students. These comments were on the work of professors, full as well as assistant and associate professors, tenured members of language and literature departments who, knowing that their work would be read by some of the most prominent scholars in their field, presumably put best foot forward in submitting to *PMLA*. And I think it is clear from these excerpts that such papers not only were not suitable for a journal with an editorial policy as ambitious as *PMLA*'s but were not good enough for any journal. And yet I would wager that most of these articles (one hopes after extensive revision) ultimately appeared in print in one of what are now more than 1,000 literary journals presumed to be scholarly. The authors were duly rewarded and the profession went on its not-so-merry way with bigger bibliographies and smaller enrollments, for if this is what was being produced for the learned journals, what kind of insignificant twaddle was being passed off in the classroom?

As I pondered these things in the seventies, increasingly aware that what was being done was, for the most part, being done badly, I began to wonder if what we were doing as "scholarship," at least in such quantity, was worth doing at all. I began to suspect that the number of articles being published far exceeded the number of worthwhile ideas on which articles could profitably be written, which was perhaps why the profession was far more cogent in criticizing its scholarship than in producing it. The *MLA Bibliography* for 1973 contained 46,652 entries. That was one year's work, and not as complete a listing as we at MLA headquarters liked to think it was. Faulkner had 134 entries for that one year, Dickens had 104, Chaucer 130, Ezra Pound 116, Shakespeare 558—even a modern writer, Flannery O'Connor, had 37 entries. My own field of primary interest is nineteenth-century British literature. I calculated that to have kept abreast of scholarship in my field by reading the 1,375 relevant entries in that single year (allowing myself to relax on Sundays and holidays and sleep eight hours each night), I would have had to begin reading a book or article every three and a half hours. That struck me as being insane. I began to think it might also be obscene.

Recognizing that there were, and still are, an astonishing number of scholars who publish more than ten papers in a single year—papers appearing like Ruskin's little glass beads rolling off an assembly line: plop, plop, plop—I even toyed with the idea of setting some kind of legal limit (as in the shooting of pheasants) on the number of books and articles that an individual could publish over a given period of time. Say, no more than one book per decade or one thirty-page article every two years, and then only after a national board of (naturally) distinguished scholars had certified that the book or article made a significant contribution to knowledge.

I fantasized wildly. What if, along with any article submitted to a scholarly journal, an author had to include a signed statement agreeing that the editor had the author's permission to send a copy of that article to a special MLA journal called *Twaddle,* a quarterly collection of the ten worst articles submitted to scholarly journals during the previous three months? Instead of a William Riley Parker Prize for the outstanding article in *PMLA,* we might have a William David Schaefer Prize for the dumbest article to appear each year in *Twaddle,* with free offprints to the author's department chair and dean. I even dreamed of the day when the following conversation could occur between a chair and a nontenured member of the department:

Chair: Smith, I've had reports that you've been attempting to publish again.

Smith: It's true; it's true. I'm sorry.

Chair: Even worse, there's a rumor going around that you're the John Smith who published this asinine analysis of "My Last Duchess" reprinted in *Twaddle.*

Smith: I did it; I did it.

Chair: How long did it take you to write that piece of junk?

Smith: Six months, on and off.

Chair: Six months that you could have devoted to something worthwhile, like reading or preparing classes or talking to students. Beware, Smith. If this happens again, you haven't got a prayer of getting tenure in this department!

I am not opposed to scholarship. I *believe* in it. I believe in the communication of ideas through print. More-

over, I believe that in those relatively few institutions of
higher education that could legitimately be considered research universities, teacher-scholars who are not engaged in
such communication are not vital, are not doing their job.
Jaroslav Pelikan claims that research and teaching belong
together, but he also recognizes, and rightly so, that this combination is "not always for anyone, not at all for everyone,
not in the same proportion for every university" (1983, p. 64).
And Wayne Booth wisely notes that "we can all be blamed
for building a world in which professional survival depends
on titles listed rather than on qualities of mind and heart,
qualities that can be realized in scholarly writing only when
the scholar has been given—or has taken—the years that
are required for learning to share a deepening and refining
inquiry" (1983, p. 321). I take this all very seriously, and that
is precisely my point. At present we do *not* take it seriously.
The reward system in the humanities, in mindless emulation
of the sciences, has forced us to play games with it—odious
games. What should be, but are not, forbidden games.

There has got to be a better way. To suggest that in the
humanistic disciplines there be a limit set on the amount of
publication is not a responsible solution to the problem. But
publication, while one way to evaluate faculty members, is
only one way, and the humanities have got to find other and
more realistic means of evaluation if they are going to preserve their vitality. I do not mean to suggest that love of learning is enough. "Cherish or perish" is not a viable alternative.
But there must be better ways.

I do not have the answer. I think, however, that if in its
reward system colleges and universities would attempt to take
a serious look at the totality of the individual—not merely
one's publications but the quality of one's teaching and of
one's mind—recognizing that they also serve who do not
always or often have something worth saying in print, we
might be on firmer ground. As a vice-chancellor I witnessed
no end of tenure or promotion cases where, having spent
months compiling incredible amounts of documentation,
well-intentioned members of a campus personnel committee

reached a decision without having seen, much less talked to, the candidate. If we were to begin by feeding deep, deep upon their peerless eyes, trusting, at times, to our intuition in appraising an individual's worth, we might have to rely less, or rely less frequently, on the printed word.

My point, of course—and my reason for laboring this issue at such length—is that the extraordinary effort that faculty members in the humanities (and in many of the social sciences) are forced to expend on what more often than not is worthless publication detracts from the time that could and should—and one can only trust would—be spent in preparing classes and working with students. The amount of time and effort involved in undertaking the research for and the writing of even a stupid article is considerable, and increasingly so as one must wade through a growing mass of previous publications on the topic if one is to make a "discovery." In returning to full-time faculty status last year I was asked to teach one of the undergraduate seminars that we require of all UCLA's senior English majors. I decided to treat the work of John Fowles, whose novels—*Magus* to *Maggot*—I greatly admire and on whose work I felt confident I could assign paper topics without compelling my students to wend their way through volumes of criticism. But as I began to prepare what I assumed would be a brief bibliography of critical studies on Fowles's writing, I discovered to my amazement that my listing included nearly 200 articles, 10 books, and some 30 doctoral dissertations (and this on a writer whose work first attained critical notice only twenty years ago). How many thousands, hundreds of thousands, of hours went into that effort, fully two-thirds of which (I read it) is not worth the paper it is written on?

This situation would be sad enough if it just ended here—wasted time and effort that could have been devoted to more worthwhile purposes. Unfortunately, that is not the case, for in pretending that literary scholarship and criticism are akin to scientific research, we in the humanities have created a faculty of scholars who are frequently so narrow in their studies and specialized in their scholarship that they are sim-

ply incapable of teaching undergraduate introductory courses.
It is not, as is frequently suggested, that most faculty are
unwilling to do so, even when they realize that such teaching
is difficult and takes time away from the publications on
which their promotions depend. More often, I suspect, it is
simply that they do not know enough, or remember enough
from their graduate courses, to be comfortable in teaching
material that falls outside the narrow range of their special-
ties. I was first struck by this when, as chair of my department
in the late sixties, I asked one of our newly appointed assistant
professors to teach the first half of our sophomore literature
survey. The reply from this young man, proud possessor of
an Ivy League Ph.D., was that he could not possibly do so
because he had never read Spenser or Milton.

This was, I trust, an unusual case, and in recent years
there has been a greater effort in all doctoral programs to
ensure that, as in days of yore, graduate students have breadth
as well as depth in their studies. Nevertheless, I would wager
that many students currently receiving doctoral degrees from
even the most prestigious universities, while prepared to
conduct graduate seminars in their dissertation subjects, are
ill-equipped if not outright unqualified to teach those undergraduate courses that are the life-blood of a liberal education.
James Sloan Allen, in an editorial published a few years ago
in the *Wall Street Journal*, expressed his frustration while
chairing academic studies at the Manhattan School of Music:
"Just try, as I have been trying, to find a young Ph.D. capable
of teaching courses in writing, 'great books,' and history in
a truly humanistic way. It can hardly be done. Candidates
come forward in abundance, but scarcely one with a properly
stocked and sufficiently responsive mind. It is enough to con-
vince anyone not already under the sway of The Profession
that humanistic education is not so much imperiled by ene-
mies from the outside, such as science, popular culture and
vocationalism, as it is by the treason of the humanists themselves" (1982, p. 30).

Sad, yes, but I fear true. As a "profession" we humanists are continuing to stress the less important—dissemina-

tion in print—over the most important—dissemination in the classroom—and in so doing are forcing our undergraduate students to pay a terrible price. Indeed, we are cheating not only our students but the society that innocently supports us and that, or so I would argue, we have no other legitimate purpose than to serve.

⚜ 8 ⚜

HUMANITIES TODAY

Demystifying the Role
of the Humanist

> How doth the little crocodile
> Improve his shining tail,
> And pour the waters of the Nile
> On every golden scale!
>
> How cheerfully he seems to grin,
> How neatly spreads his claws,
> And welcomes little fishes in,
> With gently smiling jaws!
> —Lewis Carroll

For many years I was obsessed with the idea that the major problem with the humanistic disciplines was their failure to relate the humanities to the society that supports them—a failure to explain and to justify the disciplines and to prove their value to society. During my years as MLA executive director, the one thing I wanted most to achieve was the publication of a national magazine that would help address this problem by presenting information about and developments in the fields of history, philosophy, language, and literature, and doing so with at least as much seriousness as was being afforded the sciences in a publication such as *Scientific American*. At times I thought of my magazine as being more limited in scope, a *Language and Literature Today*, but at other times the coverage was broadened to *Humanities Today* or

Humanistic American. Whatever the title or scope, I saw this magazine as a panacea, if not for all of our problems, at least for the low regard in which the humanistic disciplines were held by the public.

To assist me in my efforts I received a contract from the National Endowment for the Humanities to conduct a nine-month feasibility study on ways in which information about the humanities could most effectively be disseminated to the adult public through the print media. Although we spent the best part of a year working on that study and had the benefit of a knowledgeable advisory panel, the final report was inconclusive. Maybe a magazine was needed, maybe not. I nonetheless spent a considerable amount of time writing a proposal to obtain the subsidy that would be necessary for launching such a magazine and many additional hours talking to New York foundations in the hope that one would come up with the million dollars we needed in start-up funds. I failed.

I have, in any event, now concluded that, with or without a *Humanities Today,* the humanistic disciplines will always be of limited interest to the general public, not because the subjects are uninteresting but because those who are interested in them are too few. Publications such as *Horizon* will no doubt continue to appear and will have limited success for a limited time. The many excellent "little" magazines and reviews, usually with some kind of college or university affiliation, will continue to publish articles about humanistic studies for a select readership. And NEH now publishes its own bimonthly review titled *Humanities,* the scope of which is as limited as its circulation. But while the widely circulated weekly newsmagazines continue to devote sections to science, technology, medicine, behavior, and the various arts, there are no sections devoted exclusively to news about any one much less all of the humanistic disciplines.

This situation is not in itself either new or newsworthy. It has a long history. Were I to write that history, looking back at the relations between Western society and the humanistic disciplines since the fall of Rome, I would probably begin with medieval scholasticism and the monasteries, where I would quickly discover that there is not very much to write about. Things would pick up a bit when I got to the Renaissance and would then fluctuate (nobody loses all the time) throughout the eighteenth, nineteenth, and twentieth centuries, but I would finally be forced to conclude that, at least from the perspective of the "common reader," most Western nations have never placed a high priority on humanistic studies. When academic humanists speak of a crisis in the humanities and bemoan the fact that, at various levels of public and private life, we have lost a humanist's perspective and a humanist's awareness of our cultural heritage, it is not that we have lost but that most of us had never really found them.

Focusing on our own century in our own country, it is perhaps informative to take a closer look at the early decades, during which the late-nineties esthetic movement had come fully into vogue. For I believe that at least in literary studies the idea of art for art's sake (the "art" of fiction, the critic as "artist") probably played a more important role than we realize in separating not just the artist but the literary scholar—and to a certain extent all of those teaching in the humanistic disciplines—from society. In the early decades of our century professors in English or foreign-language departments were, of course, neither artists nor esthetes but primarily philologists and pedants, and because their studies, and all studies in the humanities, were at heart elitist and largely supported by the elite, they were viewed by society as perhaps a bit esoteric but harmless. As the century progressed, however, and humanistic studies did become increasingly esoteric, the public came to hold the academic humanist, as it held the artist, in awe if not wonder—an arrangement that academic humanists, many of whom soon joined the artists in their disdain of society, found to be increasingly comfortable.

My point is that while there has always been tension between society and the academic as well as between society and the artist, midway through this century, as academic humanists became more and more "professional," they became more and more self-centered and increasingly aloof.

Instead of reaching out and finding a means by which to share their studies with society, most chose instead to isolate themselves and their studies from society at large. By confining advanced study in almost all of the disciplines to those who would elect to undergo the tribal ritual—to get a Ph.D. and join the club—they in effect created a closed community. The humanistic groves of academe became a city as unreal as any in Eliot's *Waste Land.* Come with me and I will show you fear in a handful of academics.

Unlike the sciences and the social sciences, moreover, where a viable base outside of academe had long been established, in the humanistic disciplines it became extremely difficult for anyone who had once been admitted to the club to leave it. Employers in the "real" world had come to believe that humanities Ph.D.'s were of little or no use in the marketplace and thus, when the job market collapsed in the late sixties, many of those humanities Ph.D.'s who could not find an academic position were at a loss in seeking employment elsewhere.

In what is now a curious but at the time was an extremely influential study, Don Cameron Allen's (1968) *The Ph.D. in English and American Literature,* Allen noted this insularity but actually viewed it with pride:

> The English Ph.D. does not often venture out into the cold, nonacademic world. Faithful to his careful traditions, he enters the teaching profession at the rate of ninety-one to the hundred. The nine who stray in strange lands probably end up grading their husbands' themes. This fidelity of English Ph.D.'s to the teaching profession is almost miraculous when it is viewed against the general infidelity of the other learned professions. . . . Mathematics, Physics, and Chemistry lose from forty to eighty percent of their new doctors to nonacademic employment [p. 17].

In this passage—which incidentally reveals how much our consciousness *has* been raised by the feminist move-

ment—Allen pointed to three of the hard sciences where
Ph.D.'s have always been in demand by the cold, nonaca-
demic world. The figures he used from the early 1960s suggest, however, that the political scientists, the economists,
and those historians with a social science bent had already
successfully infiltrated society, with some 25 to 40 percent of
their Ph.D.'s being employed outside of teaching. Humanists,
and especially those engaged in literary studies, were faithful,
in their fashion, to academe.

No villain spun this plot. Humanistic scholars mindlessly emulated their colleagues in other areas of the campus,
creating exotic vocabularies and no end of ambiguities and
deep structures to prevent the uninitiated from tampering
with the sacred mysteries. In so doing, they not only failed
to make a connection between their studies and the nonaca-
demic workplace but failed to create a voice for sharing the
humanities with society at large. And although those of us
who work in the area of literary studies are perhaps more
guilty than most, the situation is not peculiar to literary
scholarship. In a recent editorial in the *Chronicle of Higher
Education*, Theodore S. Hamerow, professor of history at the
University of Wisconsin, has deplored the "serious diminu-
tion of the role of historical study in American life," noting
how through its institutionalization and professionalization
the discipline of history "has come to be largely monopolized
by the professionals, the academics enjoying tenure, sheltered
by the campus from the rough and tumble of the marketplace,
talking and writing for one another, increasingly esoteric,
increasingly recondite" (1988, p. A40). Nor, apparently, is this
insularity now peculiar to the humanistic disciplines. In his
recent address as president of the American Sociological Association, Herbert Gans has urged his colleagues "to stop talking only to themselves and start explaining their research to
the public"' (Winkler, 1988a, p. A3). And Lewis Coser, professor of sociology at Boston College, has expressed the fear
that his discipline has become so filled with "jargon, abstruse
terms, and the passive voice" that "it is quickly crossing the
line from complexity to obscurity," with the result that "we

can no longer speak to the public" (Winkler, 1988b, p. A10). One wonders how many of the thousands of humanities and social science departments in American colleges and universities have ever asked themselves the question Arnold once asked himself: "What am I, that I am here?" Not many, I think, in spite of the fact that the answer to that question should dictate all that they are and all that they do. Arnold worried a good deal about a connection between culture, or the lack of same, and anarchy. In America a century later we apparently lack a voice even to worry about that connection.

There was reason to hope that for the humanistic disciplines such a voice might evolve when in 1965 Congress created the National Endowment for the Humanities and charged it with promoting "progress and scholarship in the humanities." Surely there was reason to expect that the amendment to the original congressional act that opened up the Public Programs Division might have done it. The reason it has not, I think, is that Endowment funds for its Public Humanities Projects have largely been expended either in showing that the humanities, like the sciences and the arts, can "do" things, or in enticing humanists to address public meetings on issues concerned with national problems or the human environment. Such approaches, I feel, are all wrong. They create false expectations, implying on the one hand an invalid analogy to the applied sciences and the creative arts, and on the other hand suggesting that the humanist is some kind of high priest whose values can lead us to salvation.

It is not what the humanities can *do* that needs to be explained to and explored with the public, but what the humanities *are*, what they are all about. Philosophy, history, and literature as disciplines are not enhanced through art exhibits, museum showings, or television documentaries, nor is their study enriched through public meetings arranged by the state-based humanities councils. And yet in her 1988 report as NEH chair, *Humanities in America*, those are precisely the things that Lynne Cheney emphasized, presenting the image of NEH as an all-encompassing "parallel school" that spreads the humanities far and wide—"from reading groups through exhibitions to educational television" (p. 27). In a thirty-three-page report from an agency whose primary mission is to promote progress and scholarship in the humanities, there was not a single reference to how NEH programs had enriched our understanding of the humanistic disciplines or what a single scholar had accomplished in the way of humanistic scholarship. The report was simply a promotional piece written to improve NEH's shining tail by showing Congress how many of its constituents had passed through the gently smiling jaws of NEH public programs.

It is the study and understanding of the humanistic disciplines that are important, not the humanists themselves. Although I cannot speak for historians or philosophers, in pre-NEH days I suspect that those of us concerned with literary studies did not even know that we were "humanists"; certainly that word did not appear in flashing neon as it now does in NEH promotions. We were merely English or French or German or Spanish teachers, perhaps further identified, without a trace of humor, by our special interests ("I'd like you to meet Professor Buckley; he's a Victorian. And this is Professor Wallerstein, a Metaphysical. And of course you know Professor Frye; he's a Critic"). When I attended graduate school at the University of Wisconsin in the late fifties, there were divisions for social studies, for the biological sciences, and for mathematics and the physical sciences, but I was not enrolled in anything so grand as a "Humanities Division." My division was simply, if accurately, titled "The Departments of Language and Literature." Moreover, I do not recall that a single one of my professors at Wisconsin was ever called a humanist, nor when in 1962 I became a member of the English department at UCLA did any of us, faculty or students, so call ourselves. We certainly did not suspect that we were part of a grand humanistic alliance.

Today, however, those who teach in the humanistic disciplines—historians and philosophers as well as those of us concerned with language and literature—are constantly being reminded by NEH of our obligations as humanists and are urged, with what at times approaches missionary zeal, to bring a humanistic perspective to all kinds of unlikely subjects. During the seventies I watched in wonder as NEH allocated increasingly large sums to state programs that encouraged humanists to strike at the grassiest of grass roots by attending local meetings on all kinds of public policy issues. I noted, for example, that as a result of such programs a "humanist-in-residence" was added to Maine's Department of Mental Health and that in Oklahoma the NEH state committee sponsored a program in which humanists and prison inmates met to analyze their perceptions of confinement. A decade later, in her report to the president, Cheney still noted, apparently with approval if not pride, that the Wyoming Council for the Humanities was sending scholars into that state's rural areas "to speak on subjects ranging from the art of the Plains Indians to the construction of the Brooklyn Bridge" (p. 24). And not long ago I participated in a "humanistic" conference at the conclusion of which someone seriously suggested that we pass a resolution urging colleges to hire only those faculty members who, regardless of their discipline, possessed a "humanistic temper."

While such banner-waving and drum-thumping might be considered quaint at best, at worst harmless, my fear is that all this carrying on about humanistic perspectives and humanistic values, far from enhancing the concerns of those who teach in the humanistic disciplines, has tended to make mush out of the disciplines themselves. Literature, language, history, and philosophy are, as disciplines, closely related, or at any rate they ought to be. But the study and teaching of these subjects are not enhanced by lumping them all together along with half a dozen other disciplines and pretending that those who teach them possess some kind of transcendent humanistic sensibility that can provide an antidote to—well, to what? To scientists intent on destroying the world while the humanists preserve it? Or is it, perhaps, that humanists protect society from wicked politicians and unscrupulous business leaders? This is nonsense. No wonder, in light of such pretentious claptrap, that otherwise-well-informed people confuse humanitarianism or secular humanism or human rights with those studies traditionally defined as humanistic.

I should perhaps make it clear that my subject is not
the humanist as politician, or business leader, or scientist, or
physician. I am well aware that some of the most enlightened
"humanists" on my campus are in the School of Medicine,
not the English or the French departments. Nor am I in this
chapter exploring what the humanities "mean" or how they
can and frequently do influence the lives of those who have
no direct involvement in higher education or the humanistic
disciplines. My subject is the academic humanist, the teacher
of literature or language or history or philosophy, and my
fear is that in trying so hard to make these teachers "be"
humanists, in stressing those attitudes and values that may
(but also may not) evolve from humanistic studies, we en-
danger the studies themselves. Even the best of historians or
philosophers may be narrow-minded and prejudiced. Famil-
iarity with Shakespeare's plays does not ensure that one has
the knowledge to comment wisely or well on the state of the
nation, nor does a close reading of Matthew Arnold guarantee sweetness and light. Indeed, in this past decade I have
watched with dismay as we "literary" humanists, in what by
any definition has to be deemed an antihumanistic enormity,
have excluded the human element from the act of sharing
ideas through publication. Emulating publications in the
sciences and social sciences, *PMLA* editorial policy now
stipulates that one can no longer submit an article to this
granddaddy of all humanistic scholarly journals if that article
bears even a trace of one's identity—I would say of one's
humanity. When submitting an article, scholars must now
not only remove their names from their manuscripts but must
revise their articles to disguise references to themselves, lest
an "I" give a reviewer any hint of who they are, where they
come from, or what they have previously accomplished. If
this is an example of the "humanistic temper" that we are
urged to possess, I for one want no part of it.

My point is simply this: in pretending to be something
we are not, in pretending to be able to do things for which
we have no special qualifications, we give a false impression of the scholar rather than an accurate impression of the

scholarship. I suggest that we "humanists" talk less about what we are, which is not all that much, and begin to stress content. What we study and teach is the important thing. The best known and thought and said in this world needs no apology. John Donne's sermons, John Milton's poetry, John Stuart Mill's writings on liberty, John Ruskin's on moral values, John Henry Newman's on education—how much richer we would be as a nation were we to turn to those voices for our inspiration and wisdom rather than to the John Chancellors or, heaven forbid, the Jerry Falwells.

I consider myself to be a good friend of the National Endowment for the Humanities and have more than a passing awareness of its history and its programs. During the seventies and much of the eighties I had numerous occasions to work closely with members of the NEH staff, for whom I have great respect. In the seventies, when I was with the MLA, I visited frequently in Washington with Ronald Berman and Joseph Duffey, who were then chairmen, as well as with their program directors, and in 1973 I was a keynote speaker at the first meeting in Washington of the state-based humanities councils. In the eighties I have maintained many NEH friendships while reviewing Endowment proposals and serving on a number of NEH panels. In 1981, in fact, I unwillingly and somewhat unwittingly became, according to the *New York Times,* the "frontrunner" to replace Joseph Duffey as NEH chair, my noncandidacy having been taken seriously enough for the *National Review* to run an article ("Halt! Stop This Appointment!") that accused me—and rightly so— of having supported such things as feminist and Hispanic causes. In 1981 I also testified before President Reagan's Task Force on the Arts and Humanities, arguing that the Endowment's funding should be continued at its current level. For I believed then, and still do, that NEH has been a positive force in furthering studies in the humanistic disciplines.

Over the years I have seen NEH headquarters evolve from a modest, almost folksy, operation in an easily accessible two-floor suite of offices near the White House to a federal bureaucracy occupying half of the Old Post Office Building (complete with popcorn machines and noontime concerts). I have accepted the inevitability of such growth, recognizing that each of NEH's thousands of applicants is the constituent of a congressional representative and that each application must consequently be handled with care. Given the way of our world—and in spite of the reservations expressed above—I thus believe that most of the funds allocated to the Endowment by Congress are being expended responsibly by a dedicated and knowledgeable staff. My concern, then, is not so much with what the Endowment is today but with what it could and should be.

My fear is that as long as NEH is a political entity and its chair and the members of its council are political appointees, the Endowment will be compelled to play political games and, in so doing, will be less than it might be. We will never attain a truly national program in the humanities, much less a sustained public voice for the humanistic disciplines, as long as the NEH leadership, and consequently its direction, are subject to political patronage. Although the five people who have held the office of NEH chair have included both liberals and conservatives, they have been men and women of integrity who have served the Endowment and the humanities well. We have, however, made it through by the skin of our teeth, for each of the past four NEH leaders has been appointed only after vigorous campaigns have defeated some extraordinarily inappropriate nominees that presidents have unsuccessfully considered or proposed for the position. One is forced to conclude that, unlike the National Science Foundation, NEH is perceived to be concerned with issues that need not be taken all that seriously, that whereas one should know something about science to be involved in NSF decisions or about the arts to serve the National Endowment for the Arts, almost anyone can be a "humanist" and thus serve as NEH's chair or as a member of its council. Until we put our best selves in charge of NEH programs, I fear we will have programs that are less than the best, or at any rate programs of lesser importance to the humanistic disciplines and humanistic endeavor.

Moreover, as long as it continues to be a political entity, compelled to be all things to all people, the Endowment will be reluctant to assume an active role in *directing* national programs. In allocating its funds through peer review, it currently assumes a passive role, allowing its applications to fall where they may without any sustained effort at initiating and actually directing major programs to meet major national needs. I would like to see the Endowment set aside a significant portion of its annual allocation—perhaps as much as a third—and, with the advice of an advisory board that is truly qualified to offer such advice, each year direct those funds to solving a particular national problem. A third of its current funds could mean something like $50 million (much more if matching funds and challenge grants were utilized), and that is an amount sufficient to make a significant difference no matter how large or complex the problem identified. Were such national priorities to be established and announced several years in advance, there would be adequate opportunity for individuals and institutions to submit grant proposals designed to address the particular issue, and while under such a plan the Endowment's continuing programs would have to be reduced, they could still be continued, inevitably and not inappropriately, with an even higher degree of selectivity.

In addition to increasing public awareness and understanding of the humanities, there are no end of major issues that could and should be of concern to a federal agency dedicated to advancing humanistic scholarship. We have, for example, major needs in the area of translation, of book and film preservation, of reliable editions and research tools, of studies to improve language teaching (English as well as foreign languages) or to enhance the teaching of the humanistic disciplines in our elementary and secondary schools, and of research to explore ways through which new technologies can best be used to improve study and teaching at all grade levels, kindergarten through the Ph.D. And while NEH currently recognizes that these are indeed problems, great strides could be made in addressing them were the Endowment to devote a major portion of its effort to *directing* national programs (as frequently occurs in the federal agencies that allocate funds to the scientific and health services communities) rather than each year dribbling out limited funds in all areas, selecting what in any one competition merely appears to be the best of breed.

To a very great extent, however, the Endowment's failure to provide direction for the humanistic disciplines is merely a reflection of the failure of the disciplines to direct themselves—a problem even more critical today because of the necessity for coming to terms with those "new philosophies" that in my third chapter I have suggested are now "calling all in doubt." If there is any truth to the claim that historians are not producing a credible body of organized knowledge that could be valuable to society, that philosophers are in a state of sectarian frenzy, and that current literary theory is overblown moonshine, then surely the basic problem is in the disciplines themselves. Unless and until fundamental questions concerning the nature and the role of humanistic scholarship and teaching are addressed, a national endowment dedicated to promoting progress and scholarship in the humanities will be hard pressed to know in what direction to progress and what kinds of scholarship to promote.

What we seem to have, then, is simply the worst of two worlds. In one we have the humanistic disciplines so professionalized, so internally confused, and so withdrawn from the public that the public, quite understandably, understands little or nothing of what is involved in humanistic scholarship and teaching. In the other world we have a federal agency, generously funded to promote progress and scholarship in the humanistic disciplines, presenting such a distorted picture that the public inevitably confuses the humanities with the fine arts, with "showtime," or, even worse, comes to view the humanist as some kind of "soul doctor." If this is an accurate picture of the state of the humanities in America today—and I very much fear that it is—one can only wonder what awaits us tomorrow.

SUMMING UP

From Chaos to Coherence
in Higher Education

> I cannot really think that humane letters are in much
> actual danger of being thrust out from their leading
> place in education. . . . What will happen will rather
> be that there will be crowded into education other
> matters besides, far too many; there will be, perhaps,
> a period of unsettlement and confusion and false ten-
> dency; but letters will not in the end lose their leading
> place. If they lose it for a time, they will get it back
> again. We shall be brought back to them by our wants
> and aspirations.
>
> —Matthew Arnold

This book has a beginning but no end, although in my more
optimistic moments I like to fancy that in the end there might
be a beginning. For I believe that our attempt to provide a
meaningful education to some twelve million undergraduate
students has, for the vast majority, failed. And I fear that it
will continue to fail unless and until public awareness com-
pels our colleges and universities to determine that an undergraduate education should be *education* as I have used that
word in my initial chapter—only this and nothing more.

What is needed is a commitment on the part of each
institution—without qualification, without reservation, without compromise—that through a carefully organized, coherent
program of instruction it will share with its students what

today it deems to be the best known and thought, through time and space, in this our world. To make such a commitment is, of course, the easy part. Most institutions, without really meaning it, have already done so. What is difficult is for each institution to take the commitment seriously, to determine anew a viable definition of what it believes to be that "best known and thought" and then to establish an effective means for organizing and conveying it to its students. This cannot be accomplished by national mandate, not by the president, not by Congress, not by the secretary of education. America does not work that way. Nor is this a task that, within each institution, can be accomplished with scissors and paste. A viable college education in the twenty-first century demands a complete rethinking of what an educated person could and should know.

Although Hirsch's *Cultural Literacy* (1988) has been subjected to a fair amount of harsh criticism and ridicule (for example, Armstrong, 1988; Moglen, 1988; Nussbaum, 1987; Sledd and Sledd, 1988; and Lanham, 1988), the claim Hirsch makes in the subtitle of his book—that his names, phrases, dates, and concepts are "what every American needs to know"—at least suggests the kind of approach that is called for. The problem with *Cultural Literacy* is not that it is fascist or racist or even, with the addition of *The Dictionary of Cultural Literacy* (Hirsch, Kett, and Trefil, 1988), silly, but that those 5,000 (or is it 50,000?) "essential names, phrases, dates, and concepts" merely provide a compilation of all our yesterdays. Hirsch's "touchstones," if that is what they in fact are, may in part encapsulate where we have been, but they tell us nothing about where we might be going. If we are seriously to rethink our educational institutions, what we need is a very different kind of book—one that includes a plan for what our "cultural literacy" *should* be in the twenty-first century.

The task of definition, of redefinition, is perhaps easiest in the sciences, less easy in some of the social sciences, immensely difficult in the humanistic disciplines. But whatever the various difficulties within disciplines or groups of disciplines, the goal must be to attain what Newman called true enlargement of mind—"the power of viewing many things at once as one whole, of referring them severally to their true place in the universal system, of understanding their respective values, and determining their mutual dependence" (Newman, [1852] 1960, p. 103). The greatest challenge is therefore to ensure that the pieces are connected, that after four (or five or six) years the puzzle is complete enough to enable students to see it—whatever "it" might be—in all its complexity, diversity, and, I would add, beauty. At present, and herein lies the failure, for most students the picture is hardly discernible at all, their education being more like a series of snapshots that are unrelated and frequently out of focus, under- or over-exposed, or missing a head here, a tail there.

New approaches to new knowledge demand, moreover, new methods, and we must therefore make a serious effort to adapt to education the vast array of new tools now at our disposal. We have not begun to explore the possibilities for merging the passion and the prose through revolutionary new kinds of textbooks—"books" that, using both still and moving images, would provide not just the words but the sights and sounds of the universe of knowledge. We have hardly begun to imagine the potential for interactive computer programs in teaching a range of subjects, but especially those communication skills that are, or so I have argued, the prerequisite to any kind of meaningful education at whatever level. We must begin, if ever so slowly, to improve all of the methods by which we have traditionally attempted to teach, must replace those crowded undergraduate lecture halls in which memorization-regurgitation culminates in a letter of the alphabet, must discover a more meaningful way to evaluate a student's successes and failures.

The rewards must, moreover, be revaluated for teachers as well as for students, and in our training of teachers and in our teaching we must stress, far more than at present, the "why" of education. We worry a good deal about *how* we teach and learn, about *what* we are or should be teaching and learning. Were we to focus more on *why* we do these things some very interesting changes would, I believe, begin to occur in our colleges and universities. What I am proposing is that we completely rethink the ways in which we think about higher education—its substance and its style—and then worry about what we teach and the ways in which we teach it.

And how do we presume to do this? How might we even begin to move such mountains? During my nine years as UCLA's executive vice-chancellor, I came to recognize the immense difficulty in moving mere molehills—and even when one succeeded, the moles so often remained. One wearies. After a while "the fascination of what's difficult," as Yeats once recognized, tends "to dry the sap out of our veins." Moreover, there is reason to believe that what I see as being the most critical issue, purging the undergraduate curriculum of vocational training, is not for many college and university teachers even on the agenda for discussion.

In most community and junior colleges career education has long been a given, and while there are of course exceptions, in most such institutions one finds that "those faculty members who teach language, literature, and the arts cling precariously to the small—and ever shrinking—part of the curriculum that is left to them" (Cohen and Brawer, 1980, pp. 7-8). But even in the baccalaureate colleges, of which there are currently some 2,100 in the United States, a 1984 national survey of faculty members found only 53 percent agreeing with the statement that "undergraduate education in America would be improved if there were less emphasis on specialized training and more on broad liberal education" (Boyer, 1987, p. 107). I take heart in reading *Physicians for the Twenty-First Century*, a report written by doctors who, concerned about the way in which colleges prepare their students for graduate studies in medicine, have recommended that "college and university faculties should require every student, regardless of major subject or career objective, to achieve a baccalaureate education that encompasses broad study in the natural and the social sciences and in the humanities" (Panel on the General Professional Education of the Physician and College Preparation for Medicine, 1984, p. 5). On the other hand, one of the more depressing documents to cross my desk last year was a report titled *Strengthening the Ties That Bind: Integrating Undergraduate Liberal and Professional Study* (1988). Prepared by the Professional Preparation Network (a group sponsored by the Spencer Foundation, the Fund for the Improvement of Postsecondary Education, the University of Michigan, and a number of other well-known colleges and universities), this report, while urging the integration of liberal education into professional studies, operates from the premise that undergraduate education *is* fundamentally professional, that vocational instruction is what it is all about. I take mild consolation in noting that inside the cover of the report is a disclaimer warning that "the opinions expressed in this report should not be attributed to any of the sponsoring organizations."

In any event, I realize full well that the millennium will come—and I fear I speak figuratively, not literally—not through revolution but through a gradual evolutionary process. Such a process might best begin, as it is already beginning in a few institutions, with taking a hard look, without prejudice or fond remembrance of things past, at lower-division general education requirements, identifying at that level the kind of integrated program that could and should but seldom does exist today. In the process a precedent might be set for rethinking the entire undergraduate program and eventually for developing the administrative structures best suited to accommodate such a program. New undergraduate courses would necessitate, would eventually demand, new approaches, new methods, new tools; and these in turn would lead to new emphases in graduate education, with the vast majority of our college and university teachers, especially those in the arts, humanities, and social sciences, concentrating not as much on discovery as on dissemination, not on publication but on teaching young men and women, face to face, mind to mind, in a setting conducive to and dedicated to learning. We would have kindly *smart* elephants leading their students out of the encircling gloom of their ignorance. We would have education without compromise.

*   *   *   *

I want to conclude this book with some final thoughts about the humanities. With some 300 humanities institutes and centers on America's college and university campuses, continued congressional support for the National Endowment for the Humanities, and renewed interest within many colleges and universities in revitalizing liberal education, it might appear that the humanities are as well off today as they have ever been. One might surely be heartened if not by the single-author books that continue to flay away at dead or dying horses—my own, I fear, included—at least by the highly visible national reports that in the past decade have extolled the virtues of the humanities while calling for major reforms in undergraduate education. Of these reports, five are especially noteworthy: *The Humanities in American Life* (the 1980 report of the Rockefeller Foundation's Commission on the Humanities), *Involvement in Learning* (the 1984 statement from the Study Group on the Conditions of Excellence in American Higher Education), *To Reclaim a Legacy* (William Bennett's 1984 report, which was based in part on the findings of a thirty-one-member study group), *Integrity in the College Curriculum* (the 1985 report of a project initiated by the Association of American Colleges), and *College: The Undergraduate Experience in America* (Ernest Boyer's 1987 findings based on research undertaken through the Carnegie Foundation for the Advancement of Teaching).

These reports are thoughtful analyses of the current situation, the sober reflections of some of the most knowledgeable and deeply concerned individuals in higher education today. They differ in emphasis and scope, but viewed collectively their recommendations for reform are decisive, constructive, and surprisingly tough-minded. In one way or another their recommendations also include, implicitly if not explicitly, most of the changes I am advocating in this book. All of these reports, for example, argue for a more coherent curriculum in the schools as well as in colleges and universities, and while none is willing to go as far as I have in proposing the exclusion of vocational instruction at the undergraduate level, they all recognize the need for a stronger emphasis on liberal education with a humanistic bias. They also agree in recognizing that significant changes are occurring in the various disciplines, even if none of the reports sees this as being a critical issue, as I do. Most of these reports recognize and deplore the emphasis being placed on publication, especially in the humanistic disciplines, although none with quite my degree of despair. And most express concern over the institutionalization and professionalization of the various disciplines. Ernest Boyer, in his initial chapter to *College* (which is aptly titled "A House Divided"), provides an excellent summary of the concerns expressed in all five reports when he defines what he calls the "eight points of tension": "the transition from school to college, the goals and curriculum of education, the priorities of the faculty, the condition of teaching and learning, the quality of campus life, the governing of the college, assessing the outcome, and the connection between the campus and the world" (p. 6). These are the issues with which in one way or another all of these reports are concerned; these are the basic issues on which corrective action is being urged. Yet as we enter the 1990s one is forced to wonder whether the work of the 1980s is having any effect at all. I fear it is not—not in any significant or substantive way—in the vast majority of our colleges and universities.

There are reasons for this. One is that most institutions, when considering the recommendations in such reports, assume a highly defensive posture. Colleges and universities are more than willing to recognize that problems exist elsewhere, but when it comes to self-analysis, to relating the issues to their own institutions, they have an uncanny ability to see the issues as being inapplicable. Ridiculing the recommendations of national reports is, in fact, a national pastime, and the game is played (I myself have played it) with equal fervor around the conference tables in administrators' offices and in the professional journals of the disciplinary associations. If there is a nit to be picked, pick it. If the shoe pinches, slip it off and hide it under the table. No one, perhaps, will notice.

I think that we must also recognize that within most colleges and universities the concept of shared governance tends to break down when the issues are monumental. The faculty, which lacks the time and the staff support that would enable it to undertake careful analyses and to propose constructive change, looks to the central administration for action whenever the issue is larger than a loaf of bread. But recognizing that the chief administrator who proposes significant curricular change is inevitably attacked as meddling with the faculty's prerogatives, few presidents or chancellors are brave enough (or foolish enough) to undertake such action on their own, except, perhaps, in a time of real or perceived financial crisis. Thus most institutions simply back off from initiating changes of the size and complexity proposed here. Many faculty members are of course fully aware of the problems—they live with them daily—and the most vociferous and poignant complaints frequently emanate from those who are working in the combat zone. But to act collectively is another matter entirely, as witness the short, unhappy life of the American Association for the Advancement of the Humanities. Even with nearly 60,000 faculty members teaching humanities courses in American colleges and universities, the AAAH was unable to attract the attention, much less the dues-paying interest, of more than 3,000 individuals. After just three years, 1979 to 1982, the association was forced to suspend operations because, as James Banner, its founder and chairman, understated it, "Individual humanists have failed to develop a sense of their collective interest" (Scully, 1982, p. 1).

There is, however, yet another reason for the lack of action in these many areas, and this has to do with a genuine uncertainty as to precisely what to do. In part the uncertainty is caused by the dawning awareness that in many substantive ways technology is in the process of altering higher education. That these alterations are inevitable, are already occurring, is increasingly recognized. On more and more campuses students are now expected to own or to have access to a microcomputer, frequently with linkage to campus networks, and computers have become ubiquitous even in the offices of faculty who teach in the humanistic disciplines. But what all this means—precisely how faculties and students should be using these tools, should be changing what they do and how they do it—is unclear. When in doubt, the answer seems to be to pass, trusting that the bidding will go around once more before one has to make a decision.

Of even greater significance is the uncertainty that has resulted from a changing student population, the movement during the past twenty years tending from a mostly young, white, middle- and upper-class student body to one that is diversified in age as well as economic, racial, and ethnic background. In the humanities and social sciences the issue goes beyond the traditional dissension between reactionary and radical, conservative and liberal, elitist and egalitarian. It goes beyond affirmative action and its impending head-on collision with the concept of equal opportunity, beyond the offering of African-American history, Chicano literature, or East Asian philosophy, beyond the question of the canon and of the struggles currently being waged on campuses over requiring a course in ethnic studies. What is at question in the humanities and social sciences is the entire tradition of teaching from the perspective of Western civilization (Mooney, 1988). After all those years of studying the Greeks and the Romans, now what? Little wonder that Bloom's *Closing of the American Mind* and Hirsch's *Cultural Literacy* have made the best-seller lists, have been purchased, if not necessarily read, by some half a million. Little wonder that they have proved to be controversial, given that to many these books have represented our last best hope for preserving tradition while to others they have seemed little more than "tragedy and farce" (Moglen, 1988).

The fact is that while reports from distinguished commissions and single-author diatribes may sound the call to battle, the arena for effective action is and always has been the individual institution, where it well may be that, in spite of my pessimism, change is, if ever so slowly, beginning to occur. There are, of course, a handful of colleges—idiosyncratic and, from the perspective of the mainstream, highly eccentric—such as Evergreen in Olympia and Hampshire in Amherst, that long ago incorporated many of the changes now being called for. And, incidentally, some of these schools, in an attempt to maintain vigor in the teaching of their faculties, have even gone so far as to eliminate tenure, which is perhaps not as radical a move as one might suspect in light of a recent survey by the Carnegie Foundation for the Advancement of Teaching, which found that more than one-third of all college professors, including nearly 29 percent of those with tenure, believe that higher education would be improved were tenure to be abolished (Clark, 1986).

But while change must inevitably occur in the individual institutions, it is possible for a group of institutions to unite in encouraging new options (if not necessarily adopting the same new programs). We have in recent years seen substantive changes in policies relating to college athletics— changes brought about largely through the efforts of the chief executive officers of those institutions that have long been looked to for leadership. Some fifty of these institutions are, in fact, already united through the Association of American Universities, which, with its highly select membership—most of the elite private and many of the larger public universities—is by far the most influential of all the many national associations concerned with higher education in America today. And therein lies a tale.

In 1980–81, largely at the instigation of Bartlett Giamatti, who at the time was the president of Yale University and one of the very few humanist scholars among the AAU presidents and chancellors, the association voted to create a standing Committee on the Arts and Humanities. (Standing committees already existed on graduate education, health education, research libraries, research management, and science and research.) In 1982 this new committee authorized a "white paper" on the state of the arts and humanities in higher education—a paper that Giamatti asked me to prepare. I did. My paper, which contained many of the suggestions made in this book, was duly circulated to all of the presidents and chancellors, and in 1983 I participated in a heart-felt discussion of the issues during the AAU fall meeting. That the issues I had raised had little lasting effect became clear, however, when in 1986, just five years after the Committee on the Arts and Humanities was created, the association voted to disband it "for lack of significant agenda items." If the AAU presidents and chancellors do not recognize that there are significant issues that need to be addressed in the arts and humanities, in the liberal arts degree—and apparently they do not—I fear that higher education and the humanities are even farther apart than my book has suggested.

Enrollments in the humanities have always fluctuated, and there are of course a number of campuses on which study and teaching in the humanistic disciplines are today alive and well. Yet while W. Jackson Bate's gloomy prediction that the humanities "are plunging into their worst state of crisis since the modern university was formed a century ago" (1982, p. 46) now seems excessive, the national picture remains bleak. Although during the past decade total undergraduate enrollments in humanities courses have not declined significantly, in most colleges and universities the number of undergraduates majoring in the humanistic disciplines has decreased dramatically. According to recent figures from the Office of Education, between 1966 and 1986, when the total number of bachelor's degrees awarded increased by 88 percent, the number awarded in the humanities decreased by 33 percent. Foreign-language majors declined by 29 percent, English majors by 33 percent, philosophy majors by 35 percent, and history majors by 43 percent (Cheney, 1988, p. 4). Moreover, indications are that the number of humanities majors will not increase in the immediate future. Between 1966 and 1983 the proportion of freshmen planning to major in "English and literature" dropped by more than 80 percent, and recent surveys continue to reveal that nearly eight times as many students plan to major in accounting as in English, more than three times as many in business as in all of the arts and humanities disciplines combined (Astin, 1985, pp. 215–216).

At the graduate level, enrollments as well as the number of doctoral candidates in the humanistic disciplines are, after

two decades of decline, beginning to level off. These numbers
will no doubt rapidly increase as the massive hirees of the
sixties become the retirees of the nineties. Indeed, the next
generation of teachers and scholars will soon be hot upon us
as we enter, for the first time in several decades, what for new
Ph.D.'s will be a seller's market. Unfortunately, due to the
unfavorable job market in the seventies and eighties, many
of our best undergraduates were discouraged from pursuing
graduate studies in the humanistic disciplines, and one has
to wonder about the quality of mind of those Ph.D.'s now
entering or about to enter the job market. My impression is
that, at least in this year's hiring, there are a relatively small
number of truly outstanding graduates seeking academic positions, and they are being courted vigorously by a large number of institutions.

In sum, the appearances are deceiving. The counting
of our humanistic blessings reveals a heavy balance on the
debit side, and I see no reason to believe that tomorrow will
be better. While NEH happily proclaims that its "parallel
school" is spreading good tidings of great joy to one and to
all, while the AAU disbands its Committee on the Arts and
Humanities for lack of significant agenda items, while a faculty association for the advancement of the humanities dies
(unloved and unwanted) in its infancy, while the soul-search-
ing recommendations of a dozen national commissions rest
in peace on the shelves of our libraries, I am sadly reminded
of Cowper's "Castaway":

> No voice divine the storm allayed,
>   No light propitious shone,
> When, snatched from all effectual aid,
>   We perished, each alone.

It is easy to exaggerate what is at stake here, but to
do so, I suspect, would be counterproductive. No one today
seriously believes with Shelley that poets—or humanists—are
the trumpets that sing to battle but feel not what they inspire,
the influence that moves but is moved not, the unacknowl-

edged legislators of the world. Humanists never have been and never will be the unacknowledged legislators of anything, much less the world. But the study of history, of philosophy, of religion, of language, of literature needs no bells and whistles to justify its importance or for one to contend, as I do, that these studies must hold a central place—arguably *the* central place—in an undergraduate liberal education. No sane person would deny the importance of understanding science and technology in today's scientific and technological universe, nor would one suggest, in spite of Auden's admonishment that we not commit a social science, that an educated person be ignorant of fields such as economics and political science. These subjects make the world go round, and no one can claim to understand or to participate in this world without some understanding of them.

But these subjects, ever changing, ever growing more and more complex, are not what we take to bed with us at night, are not the things with which we measure out our lives, through which we make our overwhelming decisions. No one has recognized this more clearly, or has given better expression to the idea, than did Matthew Arnold more than a century ago. After recognizing that the results of science are not just interesting but important and that we should all be acquainted with them, Arnold continued:

> What I now wish you to mark is that we are still, when they are propounded to us and we receive them, we are still in the sphere of intellect and knowledge. And for the generality of men there will be found, I say, to arise, when they have duly taken in the proposition that their ancestor was "a hairy quadruped furnished with a tail and pointed ears, probably arboreal in his habits," there will be found to arise an invincible desire to relate this proposition to the sense in us for conduct, and to the sense in us for beauty. But this the men of science will not do for us, and will hardly even profess to do. They will give us other pieces of knowledge, other facts, about other animals and their

ancestors, or about plants, or about stones, or about
stars; and they may finally bring us to those great
"general conceptions of the universe, which are forced
upon us all," says Professor Huxley, "by the progress
of physical science." But still it will be *knowledge* only
which they give us; knowledge not put for us into
relation with our sense for conduct, our sense for
beauty, and touched with emotion by being so put;
not thus put for us, and therefore, to the majority of
mankind, after a certain while, unsatisfying, wearying
[Arnold, (1884) 1974, pp. 64-65].

This is what the humanities have to offer us. This is
precisely why they must be central to an undergraduate education. Within the teaching of the various humanistic disciplines we must indeed make a greater effort to connect—
history with literature and philosophy, literature with art
and music, and so on—but the most important role that the
humanistic disciplines can play is in connecting what Arnold
called "knowledge" with our real lives, with our sense for
conduct and our sense for beauty.

Arnold offered the consolation that "a poor humanist
may possess his soul in patience," knowing "that the nature
of things works silently on behalf of the studies which he
loves" (p. 72). More than a century later we humanists are,
it seems, still possessing our souls in patience; or perhaps,
weary at heart, we now console ourselves by trusting that
they also serve who only stand and wait. My greater fear,
however, is that we are moving even farther from the promised land, which—within my own field of endeavor, the study
of literature—is ultimately the text itself. I sense that in spite
of all the textual probing of structures and poststructures,
all the constructs and deconstructs, we have actually become
farther removed from the text and from what it attempts to
convey, have seemingly forgotten that books (or music or
paintings) were created not to advance the careers of theoretical critics but for real people who have in the past, do in the
present, and will in the future read or listen to or view them

for pleasure and enlightenment. We try too hard with something that should be easy, and in so doing we repel rather than attract those young minds that, with very little encouragement, would be more than willing to partake of what the arts and the humanities have to offer. "Through a combination of anger, fear, and purblind defensiveness," as W. Jackson Bate has put it, "the humanities seem bent on a self-destructive course" (1982, p. 46). The problem is not with society or with institutions of higher education. We are betrayed by what is false within.

It need not be that way. As I have been arguing throughout this volume, what the humanistic disciplines have to offer to their students and to the public should be readily accessible. The task of the academic humanist should be to help make it even more so. But I am of course arguing for more than this, for in the broadest sense the problems of the humanities today are merely a reflection of far greater and more serious problems involving liberal education in colleges and universities. My plea is for the liberalization of higher education, where already far too much ground has been surrendered to career orientation, allowing the liberal arts to be viewed in the minds of students and the public as the sprig of parsley set prettily beside the meat and potatoes rather than, as they should be, the main course itself. We have failed to explain not just the humanities but education.

The desire for knowledge, the longing for education, are still central to the American dream, but in failing to clarify what education means, in allowing our schools and colleges to become trade schools, that dream fades, becomes less and less likely of fulfillment. If Matthew Arnold was correct in claiming that there is a need in us for conduct and a need in us for beauty, then it is precisely in the study of the humanistic disciplines that these needs can be met and the meaning of a liberal education becomes clear. We fail to make that meaning clear at great jeopardy to education, to ourselves, and to our future.

References

Alexander, A. *Why Go to College: A Documentary Report on the Personal Benefits of Higher Education.* New York: Professional Staff Congress, 1980.

Alexander, J. H. "Education for Business: A Reassessment." *Wall Street Journal,* Feb. 2, 1981, p. 16.

Allen, D. C. *The Ph.D. in English and American Literature.* New York: Holt, Rinehart & Winston, 1968.

Allen, J. S. "The Humanists Are Guilty of Betraying Humanism." *Wall Street Journal,* Feb. 2, 1982, p. 30.

Armstrong, B. "Pluralistic Literacy." *Profession 88.* New York: Modern Language Association of America, 1988.

Arnold, M. "Literature and Science." In R. H. Super (ed.), *The Complete Prose Works of Matthew Arnold.* Vol. 10. Ann Arbor: University of Michigan Press, 1974. (Originally published 1884.)

Association of American Colleges. *Integrity in the College Curriculum: A Report to the Academic Community.* Washington, D.C.: Association of American Colleges, 1985.

Astin, A. W. *Achieving Educational Excellence: A Critical Assessment of Priorities and Practices in Higher Education.* San Francisco: Jossey-Bass, 1985.

Bate, W. J. "The Crisis in English Studies." *Harvard Magazine,* Sept.-Oct. 1982, pp. 46–53.

Bennett, W. J. *To Reclaim a Legacy: A Report on the Humanities in Higher Education.* Washington, D.C.: National Endowment for the Humanities, 1984.

Bloom, A. *The Closing of the American Mind.* New York: Simon & Schuster, 1987.

Booth, W. C. "Presidential Address: Arts and Scandals 1982." *PMLA,* 1983, *98* (3), 312–322.

Boyer, E. L. *College: The Undergraduate Experience in America.* New York: Harper & Row, 1987.

Boyer, E. L., and Hechinger, F. M. *Higher Learning in the Nation's Service.* Washington, D.C.: Carnegie Foundation for the Advancement of Teaching, 1981.

Brod, R. I. "Foreign Language Enrollments in U.S. Institutions of Higher Education." *ADFL Bulletin,* 1988, *19* (2), 39–44.

Carnegie Council on Policy Studies in Higher Education. *Three Thousand Futures: The Next Twenty Years for Higher Education.* San Francisco: Jossey-Bass, 1980.

Carnegie Foundation for the Advancement of Teaching. *Missions of the College Curriculum: A Contemporary Review with Suggestions.* San Francisco: Jossey-Bass, 1977.

Cheney, L. V. *Humanities in America: A Report to the President, the Congress, and the American People.* Washington, D.C.: National Endowment for the Humanities, 1988.

Clark, A. P. "Contract Running Out on Tenure." *Insight,* Aug. 11, 1986, pp. 52–54.

Clark, B. R. (ed.). *The School and the University: An International Perspective.* Berkeley: University of California Press, 1985.

Clark, B. R. *The Academic Life: Small Worlds, Different Worlds.* Lawrenceville, N.J.: Princeton University Press, 1987.

Cohen, A. M., and Brawer, F. B. "Reviving the Humanities: Data and Direction." In Roger Yarrington (ed.), *Strengthening Humanities in Community Colleges.* Washington, D.C.: American Association of Community and Junior Colleges, 1980.

College Board. *Academic Preparation for College: What Students Need to Know and Be Able to Do.* New York: College Board, 1983.

Commission on the Humanities. *The Humanities in American Life.* Berkeley: University of California Press, 1980.

Coughlin, E. K. "Discontent with Deconstruction and Other Critical Conditions." *Chronicle of Higher Education,* Feb. 17, 1982, p. 27.

Geertz, C. *Local Knowledge: Further Essays in Interpretive Anthropology.* New York: Basic Books, 1983.

Goodlad, J. I. *A Place Called School: Prospects for the Future.* New York: McGraw-Hill, 1984.

Hamerow, T. S. "The Transformation of History into an Academic Discipline Has Diminished Its Role." *Chronicle of Higher Education,* July 6, 1988, p. A40.

Hartzog, C. *Composition and the Academy: A Study of Writing Program Administration.* New York: Modern Language Association of America, 1986.

Hayes, R. M. (ed.). *Universities, Information Technology, and Academic Libraries: The Next Twenty Years.* Norwood, N.J.: Ablex, 1986.

Heller, S. "Experts Convened by Endowment Head Are Divided in Assessing the Health of the Humanities." *Chronicle of Higher Education,* Mar. 9, 1988a, p. A11.

Heller, S. "Humanities Institutes Signal Resurgent Interest in Field." *Chronicle of Higher Education,* May 18, 1988b, p. A4.

Heller, S. "Some English Departments Are Giving Undergraduates Grounding in New Literary and Critical Theory." *Chronicle of Higher Education,* Aug. 3, 1988c, pp. A15-17.

Heller, S. "Universities Grapple with Academic Politics as They Strive to Change Their Curricula." *Chronicle of Higher Education,* Sept. 7, 1988d, pp. A12-16.

Hirsch, E. D., Jr. *Cultural Literacy: What Every American Needs to Know.* New York: Vintage Books, 1988.

Hirsch, E. D., Jr., Kett, J. F., and Trefil, J. *The Dictionary of Cultural Literacy.* Boston: Houghton Mifflin, 1988.

Hook, J. " 'Analytic' vs. 'Pluralist' Debate Splits Philosophical Association." *Chronicle of Higher Education,* Jan. 12, 1981, p. 3.

Johnston, J. S., Jr., and Associates. *Educating Managers: Executive Effectiveness Through Liberal Learning.* San Francisco: Jossey-Bass, 1986.

Kitzhaber, A. R. *Themes, Theories, and Therapy: The Teaching of Writing in College.* New York: McGraw-Hill, 1963.

Koerner, J. D. (ed.). *The New Liberal Arts: An Exchange of Views.* New York: Alfred Sloan Foundation, 1981.

Lambert, R. D. *Beyond Growth: The Next Stage in Language and Area Studies.* Washington, D.C.: Association of American Universities, 1984.

Lambert, R. D. *Points of Leverage: An Agenda for a National Foundation for International Studies.* New York: Social Science Research Council, 1986.

Lanham, R. A. *Revising Prose.* New York: Scribner's, 1979.

Lanham, R. A. *Literacy and the Survival of Humanism.* New Haven, Conn.: Yale University Press, 1983.

Lanham, R. A. "The 'Q' Question." *South Atlantic Quarterly,* 1988, *87* (4), 653–700.

Miller, J. H. "The Triumph of Theory, the Resistance to Reading, and the Question of the Material Base." *PMLA,* 1987, *102* (3), 281–291.

Milton, O., Pollio, H. R., and Eison, J. A. *Making Sense of College Grades: Why the Grading System Does Not Work and What Can Be Done About It.* San Francisco: Jossey-Bass, 1986.

Moglen, M. "Allan Bloom and E. D. Hirsch: Education Reform as Tragedy and Farce." *Profession 88.* New York: Modern Language Association of America, 1988.

Mooney, C. J. "Sweeping Curricular Change Is Under Way at Stanford as University Phases Out Its 'Western Culture' Program." *Chronicle of Higher Education,* Dec. 14, 1988, pp. A1, A11–12.

National Assembly on Foreign Language and International Studies. *Toward Education with a Global Perspective.* Washington, D.C.: Association of American Colleges, 1980.

National Commission on Excellence in Education. *A Nation at Risk: The Imperative for Educational Reform.* A Report to the Nation and the Secretary of Education. Washington, D.C.: U.S. Government Printing Office, 1983.

Neel, J. *Plato, Derrida, and Writing.* Carbondale: Southern Illinois University Press, 1988.

Newman, J. H. *The Idea of a University.* New York: Holt, Rinehart & Winston, 1960. (Originally published 1852.)

Nussbaum, M. "Undemocratic Vistas." *New York Review of Books,* Nov. 5, 1987, pp. 20–26.

Panel on the General Professional Education of the Physician and College Preparation for Medicine. *Physicians for the Twenty-First Century.* Washington, D.C.: Association of American Medical Colleges, 1984.

Parker, W. R. *The Language Curtain and Other Essays on American Education.* New York: Modern Language Association of America, 1966.

Pelikan, J. *Scholarship and Its Survival: Questions on the Idea of Graduate Education.* Princeton, N.J.: Carnegie Foundation for the Advancement of Teaching, 1983.

Presidential Task Force on the Arts and the Humanities. *Report to the President.* Washington, D.C.: U.S. Government Printing Office, 1981.

President's Commission on Foreign Language and International Studies. *Strength Through Wisdom: A Critique of U.S. Capability.* Washington, D.C.: President's Commission on Foreign Language and International Studies, 1979.

Professional Preparation Network. *Strengthening the Ties That Bind: Integrating Undergraduate Liberal and Professional Study.* Ann Arbor: University of Michigan Press, 1988.

Proficiency and the Profession. Special issue of the *ADFL Bulletin, 18* (1), 1986.

Riesman, D. *On Higher Education: The Academic Enterprise in an Era of Rising Student Consumerism.* San Francisco: Jossey-Bass, 1981.

Rose, M. "The Language of Exclusion: Writing Instruction at the University." *College English,* 1985, *47* (4), 341–359.

Rosenzweig, R. M., with Turlington, B. *Research Universities and Their Patrons.* Berkeley: University of California Press, 1982.

Schaefer, W. D. "The Plight and Future of Foreign Language Learning in America." *ADFL Bulletin,* 1972, *3* (3), 5–8.

Schaefer, W. D. "Alphabet Soup: A Few Words of Caution." *College English,* 1973a, *34* (4), 551–556.

Schaefer, W. D. "Foreign Languages and the International Interest." *Foreign Language Annals,* 1973b, *6* (4), 460–464.

Schaefer, W. D. "Still Crazy After All These Years." *ADE Bulletin,* 1977, *55,* 1–8.

Schaefer, W. D. "Language and Education." In *Language in American Life.* Washington, D.C.: Georgetown University Press, 1978.

Scully, M. G. "Three-Year-Old Association for Advancement of Humanities to Close This Month." *Chronicle of Higher Education,* Aug. 4, 1982, p. 1.

Shaughnessy, M. P. *Errors and Expectations: A Guide for the Teacher of Basic Writing.* New York: Oxford University Press, 1977.

Sledd, A., and Sledd, J. "Hirsch's Use of His Sources in *Cultural Literacy:* A Critique." *Profession 88.* New York: Modern Language Association of America, 1988.

Study Group on the Conditions of Excellence in American Higher Education. *Involvement in Learning: Realizing the Potential of American Higher Education.* Washington, D.C.: National Institute of Education, 1984.

Trillin, C. "Manhattan: Thoughts on Changes in the Rules." *New Yorker,* Mar. 7, 1977, pp. 84–90.

Valdés, G. "Foreign Language Teaching and the Proposed National Foundation for International Studies." *Profession 88.* New York: Modern Language Association of America, 1988.

Wehrwein, A. C. "English Teaching Is Declared Inept." *New York Times,* Dec. 30, 1963, p. 23.

White, E. M. *Teaching and Assessing Writing: Recent Advances in Understanding, Evaluating, and Improving Student Performance.* San Francisco: Jossey-Bass, 1985.

Winkler, K. J. "Historians Are Urged to Act as 'Moral Philosophers.' " *Chronicle of Higher Education,* Apr. 6, 1981, p. 7.

Winkler, K. J. "Interdisciplinary Research: How Big a Challenge to Traditional Fields?" *Chronicle of Higher Education,* Oct. 7, 1987, pp. A14–15.

Winkler, K. J. "Portrait." *Chronicle of Higher Education,* Oct. 12, 1988a, p. A3.

Winkler, K. J. "Sociologists Accused of Forsaking Problems of Society." *Chronicle of Higher Education,* Sept. 7, 1988b, p. A10.

Index

Y

155